A GOLF STORY

BOBBY JONES, AUGUSTA NATIONAL, AND THE MASTERS TOURNAMENT

CHARLES PRICE

AURUM PRESS

To Tom Fazio
whose idea this book now is

First published in Great Britain
2001 by Aurum Press Ltd
25 Bedford Avenue, London WC1B 3AT

Interior design by Patricia Frey

A catalogue record for this book is available
from the British Library.

ISBN 1 85410 808 5

1 3 5 7 9 10 8 6 4 2
2001 2003 2005 2004 2002

Printed in Great Britain by MPG Books Ltd, Bodmin

CONTENTS

FOREWORD 1

CHAPTER 1: Today 3

CHAPTER 2: The Genesis 11

CHAPTER 3: Bobby Jones 39

CHAPTER 4: The Grand Slam .61

CHAPTER 5: In Retirement 77

CHAPTER 6: Augusta National 87

CHAPTER 7: The Augusta National Invitation 117

CHAPTER 8: The Masters Tournament 129

CHAPTER 9: Second World War 153

CHAPTER 10: General Eisenhower 169

CHAPTER 11: "Championship" 183

CHAPTER 12: In Perpetuity 199

AFTERWORD 225

BIBLIOGRAPHY 229

INDEX 231

FOREWORD

Bobby Jones—Augusta National—The Masters. In the pantheon of golf's immortals, these three names hold an especially revered place. To be sure, there are golfers more famous (a certain career Grand Slam champion comes to mind), courses more challenging, and tournaments older and more prestigious, but none evoke the mystique of these three, and none are spoken of in the hushed tones of awe reserved for Bobby Jones, Augusta National, and The Masters.

A *Golf Story*, by Charles Price, my friend of many years, captures that mystique. As a golf writer and keen observer of the game who covered The Masters for over four decades, he used his unique abilities and perspective to create a portrait, if you will, of these golfing greats. And a portrait is different than a photograph. A photograph captures every detail, while in a portrait the artist interprets his subject and has the discretion to include certain things and omit others. Not one of the golf writers I've known over the years was more uniquely capable of writing a compelling interpretation of Bobby Jones, Augusta National, and The Masters than Charley Price.

For reasons known perhaps only to the great man himself, Bobby Jones took a young golf writer, twenty-three years his junior, into his confidence, and spent untold hours with him talking about his life, his career, and the game of golf. In the same way, Augusta National opened its archives to this same writer and in effect told him to have a go at trying to write something that would describe why the course and the tournament are so unique.

The result is a book that stands out among the dozens that have been published in recent years on the same subject, a book that I have described elsewhere as a "literary gem." This historic book, by a writer who captured the reading fancy of golfers throughout the world, weaves together the stories of Bobby Jones, the development of Augusta National Golf Club, and the evolution of The Masters Tournament in a wonderfully touching style. It's a great and lasting tribute not only to its three subjects but also to its writer and my friend, Charles Price.

— *Arnold Palmer*
October 2000

CHAPTER 1:
TODAY

In less than two generations, the Augusta National Golf Club became the most storied in America, perhaps the world, with the only possible exception outside the United States being the Royal and Ancient Golf Club of St. Andrews, Scotland, which was a golf club before America was a country.

Of the four courses in St. Andrews, R & A members mainly play over what is known as the Old Course, which was a golf course in some form or another before America was *discovered*. Golf, as such, is therefore an old, old game, much older than many golfers outside Scotland and England are aware, particularly American golfers. As a matter of historical fact that raises some eyebrows, people have been playing golf three hundred years longer than they have been playing the piano.

When Augusta National was no more than a matter of clicks on the clock of golf's history, then, the club had already come to be ranked everywhere in the game as something of an institution, although hundreds of courses in America were older, some of which had been holding national championships before Augusta National had been thought of. As celebrated golf clubs go, Augusta National has no age at all, really.

But its history is another, indelible matter.

Modern golf is said to have begun when the rubber-wound ball superseded the gutta-percha at the turn of the century and when the British championships were monopolized by the great professionals Harry Vardon, John Henry Taylor, James Braid, and the two great amateurs, Harold Hilton and John Ball, Jr., all of them English except Braid, who was Scottish. If we look at golf that way, *modern* modern golf may be said to have begun when the steel shaft superseded the hickory in the early thirties. It is more than historically coincidental that that is precisely when Augusta National was created.

For, ever since, the history of the club and its matchless Masters Tournament has paralleled the history of steel-shaft golf.

For all its fame, Augusta National's course has little of the championship furniture you would expect to find within a course that has the status of a palace in the minds of those who fancy golf architecture. It has only forty-five bunkers, or about a third of what many other championship courses have. It has no rough to speak of, and what little there is you could hardly lose a contact lens in, let alone a golf ball. And when the course was remeasured, this time a lot more accurately, nearly half a century after it had been constructed and then embellished and lengthened in a dozen places or more, it was found to be not nearly the much more than seven thousand yards it was thought to have been.

Unlike St. Andrews, which looks today essentially as it did in 1764, when the number of holes was reduced from twenty-two to eighteen, thereby setting that standard throughout the world, Augusta National has gone through a nearly constant state of change since the course was officially opened for play in 1933. Not one hole remains as it was originally designed. The nines have been reversed not once, as some who think they know the course's history like to point out, but twice. And although nobody now alive can remember, the original design, unlikely enough, called for nineteen holes.

What has made Augusta National famous even beyond golf circles, of course, is its annual Masters Tournament, unique in many of its own rights, most of those just as hard to analyze as its minimalist golf course. The championship of the Professional Golfers Association of America is nineteen years older, the open championship of the United States Golf Association thirty-seven, the open championship of the Royal and Ancient Golf Club sixty-six. Yet The Masters carries as much international prestige as any of them and, in the eyes of many golfists, more—much more.

A few other golf events offer a first prize in excess of The Masters's. Several other events are played over courses a number of professionals, some golf-course architects, and a scattering of other experts think are far more spectacular if not superior. And the field at The Masters is often, in the eyes of most journeyman pros, nowhere near as strong as that found at almost any of the monotonous weekly events on the PGA Tour. Still, beyond the sense of any vote taking, The Masters Tournament remains the golf event that the great majority of pros throughout the world—not to mention amateurs—would most like to win.

What makes The Masters Tournament what it is—and what doesn't—is even more perplexing when you stop to think that, strictly speaking, the tournament is not the championship of anything. By winning it, you hold title to that of no golf organization, such as the PGA, the USGA, or the R & A. Winning it automatically makes you an honorary member of Augusta National, though. So you have become, in title, something on the order of its club champion but in fact something immeasurably grander. For the membership of that club includes every truly great golfer since the game was revolutionized by that switch from hickory to steel shafts: Gene Sarazen, Byron Nelson, Sam Snead, Ben Hogan, Arnold Palmer, Gary Player, Jack Nicklaus, Tom Watson, Seve Ballesteros, and so on, the list limited only by your definition of what greatness in golf is.

With the exception of a year-round office staff consisting only of its tournament director and two assistants, plus eight part-time employees as the tournament draws near, nobody is paid a salary to help produce The Masters Tournament. Most of the production, as intricate as staging a grand opera, is done, outside the clubhouse staff, voluntarily by more than a hundred dues-paying members and more than two hundred various working officials from the USGA, the PGA, and the R & A, some of whom have played in the tournament in the past and all of whom now work for nothing simply because they just enjoy being in Augusta during The Masters, sharing in its sheer perfection, being a part of the vast panoply of it all. When the tournament is over, groups of them sit down in the clubhouse and perhaps have a drink together to discuss how the event worked out. There is seldom a sense of self-satisfaction among them. Instead, they stay around another day or two to play a friendly round or so among themselves, pack their bags, and then go home to spend hours in the months that follow trying to dream up one more tiny improvement for next year's event, one more little thing, however imperceptible, that might give The Masters Tournament that final dab of polish that will say, "There! Now you're perfect!" None of them cares that virtually everybody who follows tournaments in person or on television thinks The Masters already is about as perfect as a golf tournament can get.

Despite all the simon-purity behind the production of The Masters Tournament, or maybe because of it, the event nevertheless holds the reputation everywhere in golf as being the most professionally run tournament or championship the game has known. Even people who direct golf tournaments for a living go to The Masters and come away shaking their heads at how complex everything is behind the scenes, never to be seen by the public, and how casually the tournaments committees manipulate it all, solving problems in a matter of minutes that might involve hundreds of thousands of dollars, such as postponing play or even canceling it for the day because of rain, thereby throwing a whole television network off schedule and complicating the plans of tens of thousands of people: spectators, contestants, police, the press, and that large segment of Augusta whose very economy can skyrocket or plummet with the staging of each Masters.

As nearly perfect as the tournament strikes everyone who has either played in it or just watched it, The Masters actually *does* manage each year to improve upon its labyrinthine self in some way, somehow, in a mysterious manner hardly anybody can identify, in part because nobody involved in the production of it expects or wants credit for his role, so relatively minor does that role seem when woven throughout the vast tapestry of the tournament. The Masters is The Masters is The Masters. There just is no other event in golf quite like it.

The Masters Tournament buys no advertising, does no promotion—indeed, does not even print a program. Still, it remains harder to get a ticket to than the Kentucky Derby, the World Series, or the Super Bowl. Series Badges, good for the whole tournament, are limited to past patrons who have been going to the tournament steadily since 1963 and must be bought during the month of January, two months before the tournament takes place. A waiting list for them, containing between four thousand and five thousand names, was closed in 1978. Daily tickets are now limited to practice rounds on a first-come, first-served basis, and have not been available for the tournament itself since 1967. Weeks before The Masters is to take place, the tournament committee sends out a strange request to the press. The Masters people ask the press to tell the public *not* to come to the tournament. There just isn't room for more spectators, this on a golf course that is spread out over more than two hundred acres, or more than twice that of the Old Course at St. Andrews. No other tournament or championship so loyally looks after the comfort and convenience of the followers it already has.

Augusta National could not have been started under more unlikely circumstances in a more unlikely place at a more unlikely time. The land for the course, a moribund nursery, was bought in 1931; the course built largely in 1932; officially opened for play in 1933; and the inaugural Masters Tournament staged in 1934. Those years were at the heightening of an economic depression that saw golf clubs going bankrupt literally by the week.

The city of Augusta was particularly feeling the Great Depression that, by then, had become worldwide. A once-popular resort used largely in the winter by Atlantans because of its milder weather, sitting as it does so much closer to sea level, Augusta had been going steadily downhill as a spa since the turn of the century. The current generation of vacationers from Atlanta and elsewhere had been discovering Florida, instead. Planned as a club for men only, and that solely by invitation, just one man from Atlanta belonged to the club the day it opened and only eighty other members existed, a corporal's guard from Augusta and the rest mainly from New

York City, which was overnight by train and the better part of three days by car. By plane—well, you would have to fly your own or hire one.

Those were not the most sanguine conditions under which to start a golf club. Even in the best of economic times, such a club would call for a minimum of three hundred members, all of them local residents, and each of them very active. Augusta National would have members who might play only once or twice a year, if at all.

To top off all the odds against it, Augusta National was laid out adjoining another golf course, this in an age when you seldom saw golf courses anywhere near one another, largely because the golf population of the country was but a tenth of what it would become in the next half century. This course was that of the Augusta Country Club, which was having financial problems of its own. Furthermore, its course had been imaginatively designed, although not in a championship sense, by Donald Ross, a former professional from Scotland who had settled in the village of Pinehurst, North Carolina, just after the turn of the century and had gone on to become generally recognized as America's classic architect as well as its most prolific. Anything Donald Ross designed would be a hard act to follow.

But Augusta National did. Pinehurst Country Club then had three courses, of which the most famous was Number Two. But it bore only a faint resemblance to what it would be after Ross took a look at his new neighbor in Augusta. Ross was then working on a fourth course for Pinehurst, but he abandoned the project after he had studied Augusta National. He then began to rebuild Number Two. Salvaging three holes from the fourth, he combined them with his revamped version of the second, incorporating in the process many of the philosophies behind Augusta National: broad-stream fairways, seascape greens, minimized bunkering. The result was his masterpiece, the Pinehurst Number Two that we know today, although a number of California architects transfigured it during the fifties and sixties as the resort changed ownership until, at last, it was restored to Ross's final design in 1978.

Hundreds of courses would fall under the ethological spell of Augusta National, as though it were an architectural "school," like the Bauhaus. Some of those courses had long been famous as they were, like Oakmont, whose members filled in sixty-five bunkers after some of them had played Mackenzie and Jones's version of what a golf course ought to be.

Augusta National was to become, almost from the day it opened, simply the course most golfers would most like to play, in large part because The Masters fast became the tournament most golfers would most like to win. And so Augusta National itself would become the golf club most golfers would dream of belonging to. The club, the course, the tournament would form a well-tempered triad. Together they would strike a chord in the music of golf that the game is not likely to hear the likes of again.

CHAPTER 2:
THE GENESIS

By a stretch of the imagination, Augusta National—and, hence, The Masters Tournament—could be said to have had its genesis not in Augusta, Georgia, at all but in, of all places, Omaha, Nebraska. This is how that happened.

In 1929, the United States Golf Association, which had been largely an eastern establishment until then, decided to hold its Amateur Championship beyond the banks of the Mississippi for the first time since it had begun sponsoring championships in 1895. While at it, the USGA went as far west as it could go—clear to California.

For the site, the USGA chose the Pebble Beach Golf Links, a course barely ten years old, 150 miles south of San Francisco on the Monterey Peninsula, where the craggy, pine-strewn duneland is so stunning it could melt the lens in your Kodak. The course had been designed majestically by Jack Neville and Douglas Grant, two former state champions from California, along the jagged cliffs where some foothills of the Big Sur country are chewed away by the teeth of the Pacific. Indeed, eight of its holes are bounded on one side or the other by Carmel Bay, giving Pebble Beach more oceanfront holes, and possibly more water hazards, than any other front-rank course in the world.

Pebble Beach is not particularly long, does not have overly large greens, and is not superfluously bunkered. What distinguishes it is the wind, which seems never to stop blowing there in various degrees ranging clear up to the unplayable. Consequently, those seaside holes are often appallingly difficult, calling on reserves of both power and finesse that even some nationally ranked amateurs do not have. Pebble Beach can be awesome, a course certain to evoke the heroic. The 1929 Amateur Championship was therefore almost universally conceded before it began to Robert Tyre Jones, Jr., of Atlanta—the one and only Bobby.

The complete amateur, Bobby Jones in 1929 was nevertheless simply the most stupendous golfer the game had ever known. Nobody had made the impact on golf and golfers that Jones was then making, not even Harry Vardon, the Edwardian Englishman who had practically reinvented the golf swing at the turn of the century, winning a record six British Opens with it, or Walter Hagen, the grandstanding American who ever since the First World War had been handling other pros on both sides of the Atlantic as though they were yo-yos.

Three years before, Jones had become the first man to win the United States Open *and* the British Open in a single season. That United States Open had been his second, and the British Open the first of two he would win in a row. (He did not sail back across the Atlantic to try for a third straight.) At Pebble Beach, he would be defending the United States Amateur for the third time, having won four of the last five of those championships. What's more, he was coming into the Amateur Championship at Pebble Beach as United States Open Champion once again, having won that championship for the third time just three months before. And he was only twenty-seven, leaving beyond the public's imagination just how many titles he could win before he was finished playing competitively, an end then nowhere in sane sight.

Although he was probably the most publicly admired figure in American sports and the most genuinely liked by other golfers throughout the world, Jones's mere presence on the first tee had a way of disarming most of the amateur and even some of the professional opponents he was paired against or with. They knew what he could do to a golf course once he got rolling. Even though he had lost two thirty-six-hole playoffs to professionals for the United States Open, each by a single stroke, he had won two others against them, one of which had been for this year's Open by a crushing margin of twenty-three strokes. In the thirteen matches scheduled for thirty-six holes that he had played while winning his four United States Amateurs so far, he had won by an average margin of nine holes up and eight to play, a figure that could be extrapolated into meaning that he could be expected to win one of every three holes he played without losing any.

If you were going to beat Bobby Jones, then, you had better do it before he built up momentum. Even so, you would almost certainly have to catch him on an off day, of which he did not have many. In warming up for the Walker Cup Match against Great Britain at the Chicago Golf Club the year before, Jones had played it and two nearby courses for the first times. In twelve rounds, he broke the course records for all three courses, one of them by scoring seven straight threes, and at Chicago broke his own record on the day after he had set it. Ten of those twelve rounds had been in the 60s, and none of them over par.

In the matches themselves, Jones had been drawn in the singles against Englishman Phil Perkins, the current British

Amateur champion. Jones had won, thirteen and twelve. In the final of the United States Amateur two weeks later, Jones faced Perkins again. This time Jones won by ten and nine.

After professional Tommy Armour had won the United States Open in 1927 at Oakmont—where Jones, incidentally, had played very badly, finishing in a tie for eleventh—Armour and Jones played numerous friendly matches for small sums during the summer that followed. Armour couldn't win a single match. Finally, because Jones couldn't stand taking money away from professionals, whose friendship he valued as much as they did his, he secretly began giving Armour one up a side.

Years later, Armour would tell the story on himself. Asked how he could accept "ups" from an amateur, particularly when he himself was Open Champion at the time, Armour bristled. "Because," he said, "that's how goddam good he was."

There were several things that separated the Jones personality from most if not all of the great golfers before him, amateurs and professionals. One of them was a sense of humility in a game that was supposed to humble people but very often produced just the opposite effect. This trait was extraordinary in so young a man, and it's what gave Jones the incandescent aura admired by the public on both sides of the Atlantic during a sports epoch that had—particularly in America—a lot of bright lights shining: Babe Ruth, Red Grange, Jack Dempsey, Bill Tilden, not to ignore Walter Hagen and Gene Sarazen. Before a match, Jones would offer his hand to wish his opponent luck, a courtesy, to be sure, which was practiced by other golfers, many of whom, though, picked up this bit of etiquette from Jones himself. It could be an upper-hand gesture on the part of some competitors, but Jones had an unpretentious way of doing it that left no doubt in the opponent's mind that Jones meant it. And he did.

But once this courtesy had been extended, Jones disengaged himself from his opponent's game and how he might be scoring with it, although he would be quick to compliment him on an outstanding shot. Jones simply played the course as he found it and let the birdies and bogeys fall where they may. Today, this attitude is taken for granted among professionals and by those amateurs who would like to play as well. But not in Jones's day, when match play was almost everywhere regarded fundamentally as a game of ploys and gambits to be used at every opportunity against an opponent, sometimes even in stroke play. As one internationally ranking amateur then put it, "You cannot possibly beat an opponent you can't outthink."

Quite naturally, Jones preferred thirty-six-hole matches to those stipulated at only eighteen. While he wasn't necessarily a slow starter, he concentrated only on tempo and rhythm in the early holes, saving his big guns until he was sure he could be accurate with them. Meanwhile, he worked on that quintessential timing of his, a timing so precise it made his swing look totally without effort, a "lazy grace," as British essayist Bernard Darwin called it, that had you disbelieving the length he achieved at times. And it was this uncanny sense of timing, as though he had some sort of metabolic metronome, that gave Jones the nonchalance to withstand tournament and particularly championship pressure as no one had before him and, some experts think, as no one has since. Many have thought that we will never know just how much great golf Bobby Jones had within him.

To tie professional Al Espinosa for the play-off in the United States Open the previous June at Winged Foot, outside New York City, Jones had holed a downhill twelve-foot putt with a violent left-to-right break. Sportswriter Grantland

Rice, an expert on golf and himself a low-handicap player, wrote that it was the "greatest single putt I have ever witnessed." (Keep in mind that Espinosa had already posted his score.) For years afterward, members at Winged Foot tried to make the same putt for small wagers. Few of them ever did. During a celebration of that Open Championship at the club twenty-five years later, professionals Gene Sarazen, Johnny Farrell, Craig Wood, and Tommy Armour, all former Open champions themselves, tried to duplicate the putt, just for laughs. None of them could.

Jones was acutely aware that there were also many amateurs who had the golf games to beat him in a match in spite of their awe of him—the shorter the match, the more likely. To put the situation in a way Jones himself would never have put it, golf in the late twenties was sprouting out all over with young golfers who knew they had nothing to lose by going for broke against Jones. They were *expected* to lose.

The thirty-third Amateur Championship of the USGA (two championships had been canceled because of the First World War) turned out to be historically significant in a number of ways. Most significantly, at Pebble Beach the West Coast would be getting its first look at Jones the Wonder Boy, with the result that all the preliminary rounds he played at Los Angeles and San Francisco, let alone his practice rounds at Pebble Beach, turned into exhibitions of near-mob proportions, complete with stampeding galleries and all that went with them in those days before roped-off fairways had been thought of: backslappers, autograph hounds, hand-crushing well-wishers, girls and women who just wanted to touch the young golf genius who was as handsome as many of the matinee idols who were in his galleries. Jones had to put up with these distractions between almost every shot he played.

Still, Jones did not let his California fans down. At Olympic, in San Francisco, he was the first man to hit the par-five sixteenth hole in two, all 604 yards of it. (Only one other man, a gigantically long local amateur, has since.) In a practice round at Pebble Beach, he shot a scintillating 67, including a 32 on the back nine, the 67 being five under its stronghold par and a new course record, one of many he set while in California. In another warm-up round there, he had made a game with Cyril Tolley, who was then British

Jones teeing off at the 1929 U.S. Amateur Open. Corbis Images.

Amateur champion for the second time and was conceded to be the longest hitter in the British Isles, amateur *or* pro. They were joined by Phil Finlay, from California, who at Harvard had established the enviable reputation for being the longest hitter in collegiate ranks and the dubious reputation for being the wildest. Filling out the foursome was Francis Brown of Honolulu, a high-living low-handicapper who could have been lower still if he hadn't always swung from the heels.

As Jones walked out of the clubhouse to join them on the first tee, he made some self-effacing remark about playing "hind dog" to such long drivers. Overhearing the remark was Louis Lapham, the twenty-year-old son of a future mayor of San Francisco, who was waiting to join the gallery. Half a century later, Lapham could still recall how smoothly Jones rolled his drives past all three of the others on every hole, shrugging his shoulders in self-surprise when it was called to his attention. Jones wasn't the longest hitter of his day—until he wanted to be. Then he was immense, a talent that strangely was seldom written about after his career was over, possibly because his championship record would be so mind-boggling it seemed academic to pick apart his game. He was just better than anybody else at everything.

Earlier in the week, Jones had been invited by Roger Lapham, Louis's father, to play a nearby course that hadn't yet been officially opened and of which the senior Lapham was a charter member. It was named Cypress Point, and it had been designed by Dr. Alister Mackenzie, a British physician who had left the practice of medicine early in his career for other pursuits, ending with golf-course architecture. Mackenzie was then living in Santa Cruz, on the north shore of Monterey Bay, which Cypress Point abutted on the south. Cypress Point was later described by Oscar Bane Keeler, known to everybody as "O. B.," the Atlanta newspaperman who had covered all the other championships Jones had played and who was accompanying him to Pebble Beach. It was "a dream," Keeler wrote in *The American Golfer*, "spectacular, perfectly designed, and set about white sand dunes, and a cobalt sea, and studded with the Monterey Cypress, so bewilderingly picturesque that it seems to have been the crystallization of the dream of an artist who has been drinking gin and sobering up on absinthe."

If Jones had been impressed with Pebble Beach, he fell head over heels in love with the newer Cypress Point, as though he had discovered a younger, prettier sister of a celebrated beauty. He found the design "almost perfect," oddly enough, what with his length with a driver, because of its abundance of short par-fours and shortish par-fives.

In laying out Cypress Point, Mackenzie had utilized the talents of the younger Lapham, who had the length but not yet the disciplined game of a scratch amateur. As Mackenzie stood aside, Lapham would hit experimental drives to a stretch of ground Mackenzie had marked off as the "landing area" for a possible fairway. When young Lapham had hit what he considered his best drive, he'd nod at Mackenzie, who would then walk to the ball and contemplate the remainder of the hole: where the green ought to be placed precisely, how it should be bunkered, and all the other problems he had been solving since the First World War in a manner so stylish that his admirers considered Mackenzie to be turning golf architecture into an art form.

Young Lapham was invited by his father as a fifth player to join the foursome he had made up for Jones. Although the group had tried to keep Jones's round at Cypress Point a secret, some three hundred people had somehow got wind of it and were waiting on the first tee for him.

Lapham would recall years later:

I was terrified of playing with Jones, and Bobby could see it. But somehow I got off a good drive and we were on our way.

I played miserably until the fourth hole, a par four, where I managed to hit the green with my second shot Bobby, naturally, commanded all the gallery, who were standing behind him in a semicircle. When he saw my ball land on the green, he walked out of the crowd and, in a voice just loud enough for them to hear, he asked me what club I had used, as though he couldn't possibly get on the green without my advice.

I was getting steadily more embarrassed as we played along, so badly was I playing, and so timidly mumbled something about my mashie-iron. Bobby—well, I don't know exactly how to describe his reaction. But there was no showboating about it. He thanked me in a way that made every spectator there think he had been considering some other club. Then he turned to his caddie and, out loud, asked for the same club. I'm sure he wanted to play the shot with less club, but he intentionally played it with the same club I had used, just to save face for me with the gallery. I might add, the shot was perfect. The man could do anything he wanted with a golf club. Anything.

A few holes later, Bobby sidled up to me so he could speak without being overheard. "You nervous?" he said.

"Bobby," I said, "I'm shaking all over."

"Well," he said, "I'll let you in on a little secret. So am I. I'm always nervous playing in front of a gallery. The trick is not to let them know it."

The field that would qualify for match play at Pebble Beach turned out to be filled with figures who had either already written American golf history or would do so in the future. Among them was Jess Sweetser, who in 1926 had become the first native-born American to win the British Amateur. Sweetser had almost lost his life doing so, playing with influenza so severe he had suffered a series of chest hemorrhages that British doctors treated with, of all things, shots of heroin. Fortunately, the heroin had no lasting effects, but it took Sweetser a year to recover his health.

Also in the field was George Von Elm, the amateur who, next to Jones, the pros feared the most. As a professional two years later, Von Elm would lose the United States Open to professional Billy Burke by a single stroke after two double-round play-offs. It would take 144 holes of golf to separate them by that lone stroke.

From nearby San Francisco came eighteen-year-old Lawson Little, who would win the British Amateur and the United States Amateur in 1934. Little would successfully defend both titles in 1935 for the longest string of winning matches in the history of national championships, amateur or pro. After retiring from the amateur ranks soon thereafter, Little would go on to win the United States Open as a pro in 1940.

At forty-six, the oldest member of the field by a wide margin was H. Chandler Egan, a handsome intellectual who was one of the game's profound theorists. Egan had won the United States Amateur two years in a row when he was fresh out of Harvard, way back in 1904–05. In 1910, Egan tired of urban life, packed his bags in his native Chicago, and moved to a ranch in the Rogue Valley of Oregon, more than a hundred miles from the nearest golf course. In time, he designed one of his own nearby, but did not return to competitive golf for fifteen years and not seriously until this championship at Pebble Beach.

For it, Egan had been asked by Del Monte Properties, the owners of Pebble Beach, to revise the original layout by Neville and Grant. While he is seldom given credit today, it was conceded then that the championship quality the course had that year, and has still, was due to Egan's vastly more sophisticated golf sense. Considered too far out of the competitive picture for the first Walker Cup Match between Great Britain and America in 1922, Egan would finally be selected for the American team in 1934, at fifty-one the eldest ever chosen. At St. Andrews, he helped win a point in the foursomes for the United States.

Finally, there was Francis Ouimet, who had won that landmark United States Open at The Country Club in Brookline, near Boston, back in 1913 as a twenty-year-old by defeating Vardon and Vardon's sidekick from England, Ted Ray, in a history-making play-off. Ouimet would go on to win the United States Amateur title, his second, two years after Pebble Beach.

The careers of the field at Pebble Beach would therefore straddle those of every figure who had played or would play a major role in American golf for sixty years—from Vardon to Hagen to Snead to Nelson to Hogan and, in Little's case, clear to Arnold Palmer. Of the thirty-two qualifiers, fourteen of them either had been on Walker Cup teams or would be. Besides Jones, the others either had won or would win a total of eighteen major national titles, three of them United States Opens. Jones, putting himself in a championship classification that will forever remain his own, would win thirteen national titles by himself, seven in open competition. All told, then, those thirty-two men would end their careers with a total of thirty-one of the four major national championships open to amateurs. No amateur tournament or championship could ever boast of such a field.

As in every USGA championship, there were a number of fresh faces. Young Lawson Little would be playing in his first national championship, but his face was already familiar to California golfers, especially for his cannonball tee shots. So the newest face would be that of Johnny Goodman, a nineteen-year-old from Omaha. Although Goodman had been good enough to play in the United States Open earlier in the year at Winged Foot, where he ended twenty-four strokes behind Jones, that had been back East. Consequently, few in California had ever seen or heard of him.

Of Polish descent, Goodman was the fifth of ten children who had been deserted by their father. He was brought up by his mother with help from his older brothers, not far from Omaha's stockyards. One day, when he was twelve, Johnny and some neighborhood kids ventured along some nearby railroad tracks clear to the suburban Omaha Field Club, on the opposite side of town, where, for the first time, they watched golf being played. Goodman was fascinated by the game, and became a caddie there shortly afterward, picking up a compact swing in the caddie pen by imitating the Field Club's better players and then honing his game at municipal courses.

When Johnny was sixteen, his mother died, and it now became his responsibility to support the five youngest children as the oldest had helped support him. He quit school to go to work, but the responsibility was way beyond his years. Three of the youngest children had to be placed in an orphanage and homes found for the other two. With a now still far from normal boyhood, Johnny was then able to finish high school at night while working during the day. Although he played golf only on odd weekends, he practiced at every available hour between his job and night school. By graduation, after winning practically every city tournament he played in, he was considered the best amateur in Omaha. One thing about his game was certain: there could be little he might have to face on a golf course that he hadn't already faced off it.

On the very night of his graduation from high school, fulfilling the biggest ambition of his young years, he and some golf buddies jumped into an antiquated Model T Ford and drove all night and the next day to Colorado Springs to play in the Trans-Mississippi Championship over the famous Broadmoor Hotel's course. A major amateur event then, the "Trans-Miss" had a field containing a number of nationally known players from the Midwest, notably Von Elm and, from Minneapolis, another Walker Cup player named Harrison "Jimmy" Johnston, who would be playing at Pebble Beach. To the astonishment of the entire Midwest, eighteen-year-old Goodman won it. He returned home a celebrity, complete with a parade and banquet in South Omaha. He would shortly be able to join nearby Lakewood, the Field Club having been way beyond his means.

The following year, Johnny qualified for the United States Open at Winged Foot, turning in the lowest card of the thousand entrants throughout the country who were trying to qualify for the 164 places in the championship proper. But Johnny had no intention of going to New York to play in it. He couldn't afford the train fare. At the last minute, a wealthy admirer who was a member at the Field Club and had financial interests in the stockyards solved this problem by arranging for Johnny to travel technically as a drover on a cattle car. (The USGA rules on amateur status were more lax in those days.)

Goodman's score of 318 at Winged Foot, thirty over par, was not impressive, and three other amateurs had finished ahead of him, including, of course, Jones, who won it. But, Johnny reasoned, Jones himself had been six over par, and his own score had been better than that of ninety-nine others in the field, not to mention the 847 who hadn't even qualified. (Seven qualifiers failed to start.) He felt he was on the brink of bigger things in golf. Back home, he announced he was ready to take a crack at the United States Amateur. His friend at the Field Club arranged another drover's pass to Pebble Beach.

The 1929 championship at Pebble Beach began with only one slight surprise. In the first of the two rounds to determine who among the 140 starters would advance to match play, Jones, not surprisingly, shot a 70, two under par. But his score was bettered with a 69 by Gibby Dunlap, a former Chicagoan, now a member of Los Angeles's famed Riviera Country Club, who was playing in his first national championship and, as it turned out, his last. Dunlap's 69 would be the lowest round of the championship and, along with Jones's 70, the only subpar round for the remainder of it. Nobody would break par even unofficially in match play. A bit overgolfed by now from his exhibitional practice rounds, and possibly a touch tired from traveling by train from Atlanta and then by car up and down the California coast, Jones shot a 75 in the second round when the wind came up. His total of 145 tied for the medal with Gene Homans, from northern New Jersey, who would play a small role in Jones's monumental Grand Slam the following year.

The draw for match play called for Jones, as co-medalist, to be paired against one of the higher scorers, of which there were quite a few over the rugged Pebble Beach. (Among those who didn't qualify was a maverick movie producer named Howard Hughes, whose ambition at that time was to become "the greatest golfer in the world.") For his first match Jones drew Johnny Goodman, who had qualified at 157, twelve strokes higher than Jones. It was universally conceded that Jones would walk right over a youngster like Goodman. Running a finger up and down the draw sheet, then, it looked as though Jones's first interesting match could predictably be in the third round against Francis Ouimet, although Jones had already defeated Ouimet three times in the Amateur. After that match, Jones could probably breeze to the final. The situation was a little like studying the form sheet of a stake race in which Man o' War was entered. The rest of the field had to be considered long shots.

Like Man o' War, though, Jones *had* been beaten, and by amateurs at that. In 1923, three months after he won his first major championship, the United States Open, he was put out in the second round of the United States Amateur at Flossmoor, near Chicago, by Max Marston, of Philadelphia. But, unlike Goodman, Marston was a tournament-toughened amateur who played his recreational golf over the hardest course in the country if not the world—Pine Valley. To Marston, Flossmoor looked like a playground. To make matters more relaxing for Marston, he had no way of knowing in 1923 just how good Jones was, or even imagining how great he would become by 1929 at Pebble Beach. Nobody could. So Marston played Jones not too concernedly head-to-head through the sixteenth of their thirty-six-hole match and then suddenly got hot on the seventeenth, playing the next eighteen holes in five under. It was a bit too much scoring for Jones that day; he was only twenty-one and had a lot to learn about match play, Open champion or not. He lost, two and one.

In 1926 at Muirfield, in Scotland, Jones lost in the fifth round of the British Amateur four and three to a Scotsman named Andrew Jamieson, who had played the fifteen holes in thirteen pars and two birdies. Jones had awakened that morning with a stiff neck, but told nobody about it except O. B. Keeler. It would be unfair to Jamieson to say that Jones might have been off his stick that day, but it is pertinent to mention that in the Walker Cup Match at St. Andrews less than two weeks later, Jones beat Cyril Tolley in the singles twelve and eleven. Paired with Watts Gunn in the foursomes—alternate strokes and alternate tee shots by each team—he beat both Tolley *and* Jamieson.

But that golf had been played three year's previously, and now young Goodman was up against a Jones who had since won two more United States Amateurs, another United States Open, and two British Opens. Jones was so heavily favored to win this championship that Henry Lapham, an uncle of young Louis, had bought Jones in a Calcutta pool the night before for $23,000, an enormous wager in those days. Stray bookmakers who populated golf galleries back in that Prohibition period were offering odds of two to one on Jones for the entire tournament, as they usually did on Jones in any championship, even open ones, with odds on the rest of the field starting at about twenty to one. As things would turn out, the bookmakers were being generous. Jones was a six-to-five shot to win any championship he entered.

Nine-tenths of the spectators at Pebble Beach that Monday morning formed the gallery for the Jones-Goodman match. Probably no more than a dozen had ever heard of Goodman, let alone knew anything about his background, a background that was going to give Jones the match of his life.

Jones was very nervous before the match, but then he always was, and "the more nervous," Keeler wrote, "the better he seemed to play." But, today, everything ordinary about Jones's game was going to work in reverse.

He missed every shot he played on the first three holes, and found himself three down. Jolted into the reality of the situation, the slack went out of his swing and he won two of the next three holes, both with birdies to Goodman's bogeys. At the seventh, a gem of a par-three only 120 yards long, the green lies on the edge of a cliff that falls precipitously into Carmel Bay and is all but surrounded by five bunkers. Both men hit the green, with Jones slightly away. Jones then inexplicably stepped out of golf character by putting boldly at the hole, undoubtedly trying to even the match. His putt rolled three feet past the cup. Goodman rolled his putt close enough for a "gimme," and then Jones missed the three-footer coming back. Instead of even, he was now back to two down.

Jones won back the two holes in the following five. For a halve on the thirteenth, he astounded the gallery by negotiating a stymie, chipping his putt with his niblick, or nine-iron, directly over Goodman's ball and into the cup. On the par-four fourteenth, a slight dogleg to the right, Jones split the fairway and Goodman pushed his drive into the right rough. Goodman, away, failed to get his second shot out of the rough. Sensing the kill, Jones cut too closely a bunker that guards the front of the green. The ball rolled back into the sand, and he took three to get down. Goodman pitched onto the green from the rough, and then one-putted to go one up. They halved fifteen, sixteen, and seventeen, the last with a gorgeous spoon, or three-wood, shot by Goodman. At the par-five eighteenth, both were on the green in regulation figures. Goodman two-putted for his par, and Jones's putt for the tying birdie stopped six inches wide of the hole. Although Jones's card was unofficially a stroke lower than Goodman's, for the first time in six years the United States Amateur found itself without a Bobby Jones playing clear to the final.

The golf world was shocked, and Californians considered Goodman, as Keeler would later write, "a painful accident that came over two thousand miles to happen." Bobby Jones had been beaten by a nobody. But they were wrong on one count. Johnny Goodman was not a nobody. In 1933, at Chicago's North Shore—designed by Alister Mackenzie, incidentally—Goodman won the United States Open, no less, becoming the last amateur ever to do so. Four years later, he won the United States Amateur in Portland, Oregon.

After his own shock had worn off, O. B. Keeler became philosophical about the upset. "Golf championships are a good deal like omelets," he wrote in the *Atlanta Journal*. "You cannot have an omelet without breaking eggs, and you cannot have a golf championship without breaking hopes." Jones himself accepted the defeat as he had all his victories—which is to say, acting as though he were a man twice his age. Instead of angrily catching the next train home, he decided to stay around for the rest of the week as a spectator. One factor contributing to this mature decision was that he had never known what it was like to watch a national championship.

Jones had been only fourteen when he was taken to his first major championship, the United States Amateur at Merion, outside Philadelphia, in 1916. Despite his young years, though, he had *played* in that one, electrifying the nation by leading the qualifiers in the first of the two scheduled rounds, albeit over the easier West Course as opposed to the East, where match play would be held. In the championship proper, the youngster would work his way clear to the quarterfinals,

Bobby Jones, age fourteen, playing in his first national championship.
Historic Golf Photos.

when he would be eliminated by Bob Gardner, the vastly experienced defending champion who had also won the Amateur seven years before.

So Jones would spend the rest of the week at Pebble Beach among the backslappers, the handshakers, the autograph hounds, and the giggly blondes who vied with one another in seeing who could get closest to him. Perhaps to get away from the idolatry he abhorred, he volunteered to referee a third-round match between Jimmy Johnston and George Voigt, from New Jersey, who would play on three Walker Cup teams and who had once won the Long Island Open when it had been a stop on what was then the professional tour. The match turned out to be a thriller, with Johnston winning on the thirty-ninth hole. To Jones's embarrassment, he received more applause on every green than the players. He decided to referee no more.

In the meantime, young Goodman had been put out by the even younger Lawson Little, Ouimet was eliminating Little, Egan was putting out Sweetser, and Johnston, whose health had been uncertain since he had been gassed in the war, would go on to win the Jonesless championship by first decisively disposing of Ouimet and then, in the final, defeating Dr. Oscar F. Willing, a dentist from Oregon who was one of the best amateurs never to win a national championship.

For the most part, though, Jones spent the remainder of the week at Pebble Beach renewing old friendships and making new ones, one of which was with Dr. Mackenzie, whom he had met while playing in past British events but with whom he had never had many opportunities to discuss golf in depth, particularly course architecture, an aspect of the game that had always intrigued him.

Unknown to everyone, even Keeler—who since Jones's boyhood had been his uncle-confessor—Jones had decided two years before to retire from competition after the 1930 championship season, which would be the next occasion he would have to play in the Amateur and Open Championships of both the United States and Great Britain. The strain of being expected to win everything he played in was getting to be too much as an amateur. Nowhere near as wealthy as the public thought, and still thinks, Jones never entertained thoughts of playing golf professionally. He had vast other interests and ambitions, most of them in business. He held a degree in mechanical engineering from Georgia Tech, another degree in English literature from Harvard and had quit law school after his second year at Emory University because, just to see how difficult they would be, he had taken the bar examinations, passed them, and so went directly into practice. This procedure was legally acceptable in those days, when many people got their licenses to practice law in some states simply by "reading" for it while working for other lawyers.

One of the many interests Jones looked forward to in retirement was starting his own golf club, probably in Atlanta, the members of which would be made up largely of the many friends he had made not only in Atlanta but throughout the country as well. While he knew golf strategy the way Rudolph Valentino knew the tango, and had a headful of holes he would like to design, Jones nevertheless knew there was a lot to learn technically about actually constructing a golf course: drainage, grass strains, and many other things an ignorance of which could ruin a golf course before it was even begun.

In other words, Jones knew he needed a professional architect to help him create his dream course. Undoubtedly, he had been considering Donald Ross, who was already famous for his designs. But Ross was a notorious individualist, and Jones wanted a course with *his* designs incorporated into it, not a course entirely of somebody else's. Now, here he was, three thousand miles from home, with nothing but time on his hands, and in the company of one of the world's most highly regarded architects. Mackenzie and Jones talked, and they talked a lot. The more they talked, the more impressed Jones became with Dr. Mackenzie's theories. While neither was aware of it, the Augusta National Golf Club—and, hence, The Masters Tournament—was being born.

But, looking back, its true genesis really took place in Omaha, when Johnny Goodman, nineteen years old and with only one important tournament title under his belt, decided to compete in the 1929 United States Amateur over one of the most challenging courses there is, only to find that in his very first match he would be up against the greatest golfer the game had ever known. Perhaps only Goodman could have won that match under such trying circumstances, against such hopeless odds. For who else in the field had been faced with the Dickensian responsibility of raising five children when he was but sixteen, working by day so he could go to high school at night, playing golf only on odd weekends, traveling to championships on cattle cars? Perhaps somebody else might have beaten Jones that day. But only one other man in that field ever had—Francis Ouimet. And throughout his entire career, nobody had ever been able to beat Jones twice at match play, championship or otherwise.

No, all locker-room conjecture aside, it was Johnny Goodman, from Omaha, who had beaten Bobby Jones earlier than he had ever been beaten in the Amateur, and Jones had been playing in it since the age of fourteen. If this defeat had not taken place practically at Alister Mackenzie's doorstep, it seems safe to say that Augusta National would not be the Augusta National we know today. As O. B. Keeler was to write

Dr. Alister Mackenzie in full Scottish regalia. Historic Golf Photos.

so often of Jones's career, what characterized it most was its aura of "predestination."

Then fifty-nine, Alister Mackenzie had led a checkered and slightly mysterious career. It has always been universally presumed that he was Scottish, when, in fact, he was born in Birmingham, England. (His father was Scottish and his mother was English.) But he played his Scottish ancestry to its commercial hilt, often wearing kilts to formal affairs instead of tuxedos, and sometimes wearing one on what could be considered no occasion at all. The most widely printed photographic portrait of him has him wearing a kilt as though he were some latter-day Robert Burns. To this day, moreover, his name is more often than not misspelled with a capital K, an error due to the peculiarly large way he formed the letter k in his signature. But in an obscure book he had published in 1920, he spells his name with a lower-case k, although it was spelled both ways in some legal papers pertaining to him.

In the First World War, Mackenzie had served as a major in the medical corps of the British army, but somehow had himself transferred to a camouflage unit, where some of his ideas proved ingenious. A keen golfer all his life, he abandoned medicine forever after the war to try his hand at course architecture, a field in which he proved to be not only ingenious but something of a classicist as well. He could somehow take a mundane tract of land and turn it into a golf course that, while not spectacular, sooner or later began to grow on you. (Cypress Point is certainly spectacular, but the land was spectacular before Mackenzie ever stepped foot on it.)

Few club members who played over a Mackenzie-built course ever resigned. It wasn't a matter so much of what he put into his courses as what he left out, as is true of any artistic achievement, from a sculpture to a poem to a sonata. "A good golf course," he told Jones, "is like good music. It isn't necessarily a course which appeals the first time you play it." Jones, an opera buff, liked that observation. The first time he had played the Old Course at St. Andrews, he hated it. Eventually, it became the course he loved most.

Mackenzie eschewed rough just for the sake of rough, particularly when it was cut in a straight line, as though it were sidewalks on either side of a street. He thought there was entirely too much of it on most courses, often serving no strategic purpose and too often slowing up play. Jones, who wanted a course that would be fun for members as well as a test for pros, cottoned to this idea.

As they walked Pebble Beach together for the rest of the week, Mackenzie went on to say that a course should look "much more difficult than it really is." That theory, too, fitted in with Jones's plan for his 90-shooter friends.

Mackenzie went on to say that any golf course worth playing should have "a spirit of adventure." By that he meant it shouldn't be featureless, look manufactured, or make the futile attempt to eliminate the element of luck in golf. Nothing—no tree, no water hazard, and especially no bunker—should be placed where it would be expected to be. "Excellence of design," he said, "is more felt than fully realized." Jones, whose favorite course in all the world was St. Andrews—that enigma wrapped in a mystery—knew then that he had found his architect. All he had to do now was find a suitable site for the golf course.

Of course, Jones had that one last year of championship golf in front of him, a campaign that would take place on both sides of the Atlantic and include the Open and Amateur Championships of both the United States and Great Britain.

Only once before had he attempted to play in all four during the same year.

Before Jones came along, no one had so much as entertained the thought that anyone could win them all over any span of years. But now Jones had won each of them at least twice, except the British Amateur, which he had never won, having been defeated in the fifth round in 1926 on the only occasion he had to enter it. That someone might win all four championships in a single season—two seventy-two-hole open championships and thirteen straight matches in amateur championships—was to think in terms of exploring the moon in an age when almost everybody still believed the world was flat. O. B. Keeler would eventually label the feat the Grand Slam, taking his cue from contract bridge, the game that was sweeping the nation. But that name would not be tagged onto the feat by the public until after it had been done. In 1929, a name in golf for what Jones was about to explore would be historically impossible. That territory had yet to be discovered. As a golfer, Jones was about to walk on alien earth.

In the meantime, Jones had little reason to be optimistic about his ideal golf course at an ideal club. He had no name for it, no ground to build it on, and no members to join when he did. Indeed, he was not even sure where it ought to be—just someplace in Georgia, preferably near Atlanta.

CHAPTER 3:
BOBBY JONES

Nobody before or since Bobby Jones, and nobody except him, could have established the Augusta National Golf Club, engineered its golf course, so architecturally ahead of its time, and inspired The Masters Tournament, an event that was conceived by him as little more than an outing among his past amateur and professional competitors and which then escalated on such a grand scale that—in hardly any time at all by the game's gray-beard standards—it became indistinguishable in the public mind from a national championship. To understand why nobody but Jones could have brought off such an enterprise—the trinity of club, course, and tournament—is first to understand who Bobby Jones was in the context of golf's long, long history. For, even half a century after his retirement, no more than a handful of golfists fully comprehended Jones and what he had done, despite his fame, etched as it was in marble.

Jones's historical career straddled the eight years from 1923 through 1930, part of an intoxicating era labeled the "Jazz Age," which was romantically chronicled by novelist F. Scott Fitzgerald, whom Jones never met but whose life would be curiously touched by Jones. The era, though, was not altogether as gossamer as Fitzgerald wrote of it. During that period, newspapers were full of stories about cloudy figures doing strange things that the public found hard if not impossible to understand. Pablo Picasso was baffling the eye with Cubism. Sigmund Freud was explaining the human mind with a lot of Greek about the id, the ego, and the superego. Albert Einstein was an ultrahighbrow who claimed that space was not infinite, that parallel lines *did* meet eventually, and that the shortest distance between two points was *not* a straight line.

The world was going crazy, and at this heady hour of history Bobby Jones came along.

Actually, society was leaving what the art-scientific community today calls the "see-touch" realm of experiencing things. Art would no longer be just a formal assemblage of shapes and colors with reference to something in nature, but largely nonrepresentational; "abstract," the public would call it. We were finding new ways of perceiving things. Euclidean geometry and Newtonian physics had been made obsolete, and so we were finding new ways of measuring things.

Few athletes then, or now, were aware of the revolutions in thought taking place. But Jones was. While he was no intellectual in the European sense—and certainly not in the egghead connotation that Americans attached to the word—he had had his scientific mind toughened at Georgia Tech, where he had received high marks in, besides engineering, such subjects as mathematics, chemistry, geology, and physics. He expanded his artistic sense at Harvard by studying French and German, both ancient and nineteenth-century European history, as well as his major, English literature, in which he concentrated on John Dryden, Jonathan Swift, and William Shakespeare. After Harvard, he would read Henry James, Herman Melville, and Joseph Conrad while most of his Georgia Tech friends would be cerebrally content with—well, F. Scott Fitzgerald.

In the meantime, the public was looking upon Jones, as much of it still does, as a rich amateur (although his father was only a moderately successful lawyer) who would win a lot of big tournaments, some of them somehow against professionals, because he didn't do anything but play golf. Then, at the peak of his career, he would quit competitive golf to turn professional—naturally. But for a reason that few people then (and even fewer now) could make any sense of, he would never play golf for money.

It was crazy.

That was how much of the public saw him then, and that is unfortunately how much of it would see him thereafter. But that wasn't Bobby Jones at all.

As with so many historical figures of that age, it has been difficult for the public to bring Jones into focus, into some meaningful sports perspective, if he is to be viewed just as a sports figure. In playing one of the most complex games ever devised, though, it should have been seen then and must be said now that Bobby Jones was transcending sports. As a result, nobody then was altogether sure what Jones was doing when he was doing it, perhaps not even he himself. And few persons today, because of the dimensionless way he has been looked at, are altogether sure what he did, now that it is historically taken for granted.

Even harder is to try to explain it.

To understand Jones's career properly, one must view it in dimensions, and not just the standard three dimensions, but four. For there was the dimension of time-space to it, a dimension incomprehensible during the "see-touch" age, an era that could revel in airplanes, now that the Wright Brothers had ended the age-old search for powered flight, but thought a Picasso, a Freud, an Einstein was nuts.

Francis Ouimet (right), here pictured with Walter Hagen, was one of America's first great amateurs—and a lifelong friend of Jones's.
Historic Golf Photos.

Bobby Jones and the brief, brilliant golf he played occupied a unique space in the game's history, in the more than five centuries that we can be certain it was played before he came along. As the century advanced, one man's "abstract" art would become another man's graffiti, psychoanalysts could be found in the Yellow Pages, and Einstein, whose name had become synonymous with nuclear fission and extraterrestrial flight, among other offspring of his physical world unimaginable back in the twenties, would have his likeness printed on schoolboy T-shirts, just like Elvis Presley's. Looking back from that vantage point, it would have to seem as though, in golf, time had stood still for Bobby Jones.

Jones and his golf were not simply part of the game's continuum. He did not just pick up the torch where other golfers had historically left off—such as Harry Vardon, who had won six British Opens and a United States Open before Jones reached manhood. That role could more aptly be said to have been filled by Walter Hagen, who was as American as Babe Ruth and whose golf would overlap Vardon's by his winning eleven national championships, including four British Opens, in a career that started when Jones was a boy and did not end until after Jones had retired.

Nor did Jones hand a torch over to anybody else; say, Sam Snead, Byron Nelson, or Ben Hogan, although he was only ten years older than they, all three having been born in 1912, Jones on St. Patrick's Day, 1902. Jones was an amateur in every unsullied sense of that today much-abused word. They were professionals, thoroughly so, cast in an heroic mold of their own that was in an utterly different socioeconomic world. In it, they would pioneer the PGA Tour as we know it today, with all the glamour, glitter, and gigabucks it has going for it. Although he was an honorary vice president of the

Professional Golfers Association from 1931 till he died, Jones was never part of their world. To this day, The Masters Tournament uses its own method and not the PGA Tour's for inviting contestants. The reason is not that Jones was antiprofessional, as some pros still persist in thinking, but because it was amateur golf he sprung from and it was amateur golf he wanted to see perpetuated.

Although Jones was an amateur, and one in its purest form, being an amateur was only part of his uniqueness. When, at the age of twenty-one, he won his first "big tournament," the United States Open, he had not written any history. Three of the eight previous Open Championships had been won by amateurs, and two of the eight by younger men. (No championships were held in 1917 or 1918 because of the war.)

In 1913 at The Country Club in Brookline, in greater Boston, amateur Francis Ouimet, a twenty-year-old former caddie, had accomplished what would later seem an historic feat, but in 1913 did not cause a nationwide sensation, mainly because there were not more than 300,000 golfers in the whole country. Having implausibly tied Vardon and Vardon's long-driving shadow, Ted Ray, for the Open Championship, Ouimet then went out and not only beat the two of them the next day in an eighteen-hole play-off, he nearly beat their better ball.

Francis Ouimet—whose name was pronounced WE-met—was a genuinely modest, self-effacing hero who, unlike many British and American champions then, did not have to be sanitized by the press or anyone else. Francis the Champion drank, and preferred to drink, ginger ale, for instance, in a game that had more than its share of two-fisted drinkers of alcohol. Even the always civil Vardon was not disinclined to drinking before an exhibition, and Ray was not above brawling in barrooms after one. No one criticized them for such behavior, because their actions were not considered exceptional. But in such company, Francis, soda pop in hand, seemed like Tom Swift by comparison. Added to his incredibly exemplary behavior was the fact that he was not, strictly speaking, a country-club amateur; he was a gentleman among men who were supposed to be gentle but who, in reality, not always were. Thus, he removed the country-club stigma from amateur golf by making it apparent to those nongolfers who might not otherwise have taken up the game that you did not have to be a plutocrat in order to play golf and play it well. Finally, there was the much-publicized fact that Francis was a former caddie, and nobody can even guess how many youngsters that background inspired. For almost forty years after Ouimet, every American professional and amateur golfer of note, with only a handful of exceptions, came up from the ranks of caddies. Ouimet would become a lifelong friend of Jones's.

Two years later, after Hagen had won the first of his two United States Opens, the championship was won over what is now the Upper Course at Baltusrol, in New Jersey, by a playboy amateur named Jerry Travers. But Travers's win was not considered the stuff of which headlines are made. Playboy or not, he was known as a streetfighter in competition, having already won the United States Amateur four times. Travers would not defend his Open title and, after the war, would become a teaching professional. He would watch Jones's career from the sidelines, stupefied by it all.

The year after Travers, the Open Championship would again be won by an amateur, this time by Charles "Chick" Evans, Jr., of Chicago, who, like Ouimet, had been a caddie.

Where Ouimet had been retiring, almost bashful, though, Evans was ebullient, always laughing and joking with the galleries and calling out an endless spiel of first names with the studied abandon of a tractor salesman. Using only seven clubs, he established at Minikahda, near Minneapolis, a scoring record of 286 that would stand for twenty years. Three months later, at Merion, on Philadelphia's suburban Main Line, Evans would win the United States Amateur as well, becoming the first to win both championships in the same year. In the field was Bobby Jones, aged fourteen, playing in his first major championship. Even then, he could drive 250 yards. He got national attention right off, leading the first qualifying round. Evans would be struck with young Jones's concentration "of the most perfect kind," as though Jones were stating out loud that "no outside interest shall interfere," that golf is "a hard, stern business."

Although Evans undoubtedly didn't realize it, he was paraphrasing precisely the quality that philosopher-psychologist William James had said identifies people of genius. And perhaps in the final analysis that is what separated Bobby Jones from all other golfers. He simply had a genius for the game.

From 1923 through the 1929 Amateur Championship at Pebble Beach, the public was beginning to measure in its mind the length of Jones's career. Having no way of knowing Jones had planned to retire in 1930—and probably unable to believe that plan even if they had—golfers everywhere could see no end to it. That was the first dimension of Bobby Jones and his golf, its length. With no end in sight, he cut off his career while the see-touch world around him, whose yardsticks were Vardon and Hagen, was beginning to make wild guesses about how many championships he would win ten or a dozen years into the future.

But that was only the length. The height was something else.

Tournament golf is to ordinary golf what walking a tightrope is to walking along the ground. You have to watch your step. No longer are putts conceded "inside the leather." You must play the ball as it lies, not roll it over. And you must play all the Rules of Golf, some of which you may not have come up against before or, if so, ignored.

But in tournament golf, relatively speaking, the rope is only six feet off the ground. In *championship* golf, they raise the rope to sixty feet. Golfers who at six feet off the ground could do handstands, pirouettes, and back flips, now find that they can't even walk across it.

National championship golf—to go as high in golf as you can go—is when they throw the net away. What's more, you are playing under the glare of a spotlight, the whole world waiting breathlessly to see what mistakes you might make. In such circumstances, you often have to feel your way with hyper-developed instincts. Either that, or be awfully lucky.

Bobby Jones was not just lucky. At that height and under that spotlight, he had had no equal before him, none during his time, and, some golfists think, none since then. In the see-touch realm of experience, it was possible to measure what everybody had done on a championship scale before him, such as Vardon, or during his time, such as Hagen. But only in the enlightened world that would follow Jones would it be equally possible to measure what anybody would do after him, such as Ben Hogan or Jack Nicklaus, the only two golfers since mentioned in the same breath with Jones. The see-touch measurements became specious; empty by whatever historical method you used, and certainly meaningless by taking Jones or Vardon or Hogan or Nicklaus out of the context of their own times. How could you compare Napoleon Bonaparte with, say,

Douglas MacArthur? Or either of them, looking back, to Alexander the Great?

Jones's vintage years were scant, covering only a period of time it takes today for most young pros to win a single tournament. But the record he set in those eight years was colossal. He was so thoroughly cultivated as a golfer that merely by beating him once, even a professional could gain for himself a degree of fame that would follow him for the rest of his days.

Jones did not win every major championship he played in. It just seemed each time that he should have. When he didn't win, he made news because he didn't. Jones lost two United States Opens in play-offs, and the news of those events was that he had lost, not that somebody else had won. He finished three strokes behind the winner of another United States Open and eight strokes back in still another, and still the news was that Jones had not won. In the 1927 Open at Oakmont, where he finished in eleventh place and eight strokes back, accounts of the event either implied or stated outright that there was something wrong with the golf course. (Some people still think there was.)

From 1923 on, then, it was Jones against anybody; Jones against everybody; Jones, in fact, against the field. So completely did he disconcert the opposition, amateur or pro, that any other golfer finding himself anywhere near contending for a title reacted to the situation by picking up his head and asking, "What's Jones doing?" Beat Bobby, so the thinking went, and you had to win.

Mathematically, that thinking was correct. From 1923 through 1930, Jones won thirteen of the twenty-one major national championships he played in, or 62 percent of them. By bookmakers' standards, you could win money by giving six-to-five on Jones against the whole world.

Jones won five of eight United States Amateurs, and was runner-up in another. He established a long, long string of records for that championship, eighteen of which still stand. He also won one of the two British Amateurs he played in. But amateur championships then or now could never contain the golf that Jones played and, consequently, could never bring him into focus. In a thirty-six-hole match, it was even money that no amateur in the world could last past the thirtieth hole against him.

In *open* competition, however, you could begin to see how gigantic a golfer Jones truly was. In eleven of the last twelve Open Championships he played in, either in the United States or Great Britain, he finished no worse than second, winning seven of them. In 1926, he was the first man ever to win the Open Championships of both countries, for which New York City gave him a parade up Broadway. Inarguably, the best professionals in America if not the world then were Hagen and, to an extent he was yet to realize, Gene Sarazen. From 1923 on, neither of them ever won a championship that Jones entered. As a matter of record, Jones lost two of the four play-offs he was in for the United States Open to professionals nobody had thought had any chance against Jones head-to-head, perhaps not even they themselves.

It's a small wonder that the public couldn't see the length and height of Jones's career during it. There were too many trees in his forest. Even today, looking at it with the advantage of time, it looms taller and taller, wider and wider.

Then, but by no means last, came the depth of Bobby Jones and his golf.

From scanning his record, you had to get the impression that Jones did little or nothing except play golf. How else could he so consistently outplay the pros? But just the opposite was the truth. At the peak of his career, when Jones himself must have known as well as everybody else that he was unquestionably the best golfer in the world, he never regarded the game as anything more or less than what it is—a game. "My wife and my children came first," he would say in later years, then my [legal] profession. Finally, and never in a life by itself, came golf." As proof of this attitude, there were the time-consuming activities in his life. After graduation from high school at sixteen, he had been earning those degrees from Georgia Tech and Harvard. Then he spent the two years at Emory University before passing the bar exams, after which came the practice of law itself. During the winter of 1926, he had dabbled in a Florida real-estate venture, which he found boring, and had undergone a humiliating defeat at the hands of Hagen, twelve and eleven, during an exhibition match scheduled for seventy-two holes. But his game had been rusty.

It's a small wonder. Because of his outside activities, Jones averaged no more than three months a year playing in, and going to and from, championships. Mere tournaments were just a sideline with Jones, used mainly to warm up his game for national championships after long layoffs. From 1923 through 1930, he played in only seven nonchampionship tournaments, five of which were in open competition. Still, rusty as he had to be, he won four of them. Except for the three years when he journeyed to Britain, most of the competitive season was spent quietly at home, where he devoted no more time to golf than the average doctor, averaging about eighty rounds a year. Without doubt, Jones played less formal golf in the eight years of his championships than any other first-rank golfer in the world.

Jones never took a formal golf lesson in his life. He had put the basics of his game together by mimicking Stewart Maiden, the Scottish pro at East Lake, his club in Atlanta. Maiden was known as "Kiltie the Kingmaker" for his work with promising youngsters. But Jones's swing as he matured became distinctly his own, the quintessence of what professionals taught but often couldn't bring off themselves, what with its grace, its panther power, its balletic balance. Bernard Darwin would write that it had "a touch of poetry."

What did the Jones swing look like? Well, if you hadn't positioned yourself in the gallery soon enough to see him pluck the club that he was going to use from his bag, you might miss the swing altogether, so free was his shot-making of pre-liminary nonsense. Having thoroughly thought out the shot as he walked to his ball, he chose his club after only one quick look at his target to confirm his thinking. He never asked his caddie for advice, and he may have been the first to say in golf that "if I had to ask a caddie what club to use, I'd carry the bag and let him play."

Jones then took his stance with the nonchalance of a man about to lop off the head of a dandelion. His feet were fright-fully close together, so close even with a driver that you had to wonder how he could maintain his balance. With short-irons, his heels almost touched one another, and with pitches, chips, and putts they actually did. His arms hung limply from his shoulders as he bent over ever so slightly toward the ball, his spine arrow-straight. With only one cur-sory glance at his target, he then went into his backswing with no waggle whatsoever and only a suggestion of a for-ward press. Almost immediately, he began the turn of his hips and shoulders, the fullest pivot perhaps the game has known. It was all done so slowly that he seemed reluctant to take the clubhead away from the ball, and in fact it did not leave the ball until a straight line existed between his left shoulder clear down the shaft to the ball. Then the clubhead seemed to drag away until he reached the top of his back-swing, where the club was taken past the line parallel to the ground, as almost everybody had to do with hickory shafts in order to generate clubhead speed.

It was at this stage that the "poetry" began. Just as the shaft went past parallel, the clubhead pointing to the right of his tar-get, Jones had already simultaneously begun turning his hips for the downswing. Others, even professionals, tried to imitate the "flow" with which he somehow could begin his downswing with the lower half of his body before the upper half had fin-ished the backswing, but nobody could ever quite capture the essence of it. As the clubhead approached the ball, there was never any suggestion by Jones of hitting the ball. Instead, he seemed to just "pour" the clubhead through the ball, as though it were not there, which is what Darwin meant by "lazy grace," finishing with an effortless follow-through that left him per-fectly balanced on his left leg, the inside of his right foot adding a token of support. You could place a ruler on the line that existed from his head, through his shoulders, and down his entire left side. Very often, Jones started to walk toward his ball from this position, just letting the club fall in his right hand to his side as he did so. He wasn't showing off. By the time he had reached the finish of his follow-through, galleries had pushed past the marshals and were almost atop him.

So utterly without effort was his entire swing that newsreels of his championships gave the impression they had been made in slow motion. When he first saw Jones play a shot, Darwin was standing behind a green that Jones was playing a short-iron to. "I didn't think the ball would get halfway to the green," Darwin would recall. But it did, dropping to the green as though it were tied to a parachute, and then spun to a stop hole-high.

Jones never varied the no-nonsense manner with which he played golf shots, whether they were for a dollar against some duffer friend or for a national championship. What was the secret to this almost indecent relaxation? For one thing, there was his uncluttered concentration. "I never think of anything at the address except hitting the ball," he said. "If I don't, I don't hit the ball." Then there was his grip, which, he explained, "should be no firmer than it would while shaking hands with a lady." With his putter, that grip was even more delicate. "You ought to be able," he said, "to kick the putter out of your hands at any time just by tapping it with the toe of your shoe."

The thinking behind Jones's swing was eminently his own, a lot of which he wrote about in a series of pearl-like essays that were nationally syndicated in the nation's newspapers when such a practice was not against the regulations of amateur status. (Jones had an agreement with the United States Golf Association, which *he* insisted on, that called for him to do the actual writing himself, not with a "ghost." Contrary to what the public thought, O. B. Keeler had nothing to do with the columns.) Thirty years later, Jones would skim off the cream of them for a book, entitled, simply and directly enough, *Bobby Jones on Golf*. There wasn't a bromide in it. Golfers who had read dozens of how-to books before Jones's book were amazed at how much of what their authors had said had already been said by Jones. Either that, or they were set back by how much of what they had read no longer made sense after reading what Jones had to say on the same subject.

To illustrate, it had been argued about putting for years that if you were never up, you were never in. The theory seemed sound enough on the surface but, after mulling it over, Jones rejected it as sophistry. "Of course," he said, "we never know but that the ball which is on line and stops short would have holed out. But we *do* know that the ball that ran past *did not* hole out." Thereafter, Jones played his putts to "die" at the hole. To the ordinary tournament player, such technical hair-splitting might have seemed ridiculous. But Jones wasn't a tournament player. He was a *championship* player.

For the technocrats who can only view golf's history in the dimension of scoring, Jones's scores prove he had little more respect for par than pros do today. While warming up for the Walker Cup Match at the Chicago Golf Club in 1928, he established the course record at nearby Old Elm the first time he played it. A few days later, he broke the course record at Chicago. The following day, he broke *that* record and tied the old one the day after. A few days later, while playing in a local invitation tournament—which he won—he broke the course record at Flossmoor, despite having played the first seven holes in two over par. He finished 3, 3, 3, 3, 3, 3, 3, 4, 3, 4, 4. After three more rounds, someone added up Jones's last dozen rounds. They came to this: 69, 71, 69, 68, 68, 68, 67, 68, 67, 70, 69, 67. It should be kept in mind that Jones played with hickory shafts and used a ball that was easily thirty yards shorter than today's, all over courses that were in atrocious condition by current standards, and before numerous changes were made in the Rules, such as cleaning the ball on the green, which in themselves would make scoring measurably easier.

Above and beyond his golf game, there was something about Jones himself that everybody immediately liked, whether they knew him or not. His humility, which he did not wear on his sleeve, had a lot to do with this mass empathy. While at Harvard, he was ineligible for the golf team because he had already matriculated at Georgia Tech. So he offered to serve as the team's manager. Informed by nonplussed officials that the team already had one, Jones then offered to serve, and did, as assistant manager, this at a time when he was Open Champion of his country. "How else was I going to get a crimson *H*?" he would explain years later when the almost laughable job was brought to his attention.

Although he beat the pros of both America and Great Britain with what should have been embarrassing regularity, they placed him on a pedestal that amounted to adoration. Professional Orville White, who would eventually retire near Augusta, was one of the hundreds of pros who would end up looking upon the Jones technique in awe. "When Bob was playing down a parallel fairway," he would say years later, "we all stopped what we were doing. You just could not play golf when you had the chance to watch him. He was just—well, like no one we had ever seen.

"What was the best part of his game? All of it. Christ, he was long! He was the greatest putter who ever lived. Nobody could do with irons what he did with them. And he's the only man I ever saw who could back up a three-wood on a green."

Off the course, Jones was as much loved by the pros as he was on it. He could drink with Ted Ray or Tommy Armour or Walter Hagen, or be just as likable not drinking at all with Francis Ouimet. Yet there was nothing calculating or priggish about his behavior. He smoked to excess on the course, drank corn whiskey off it, swore magnificently in either place, and could listen to, or tell, an off-color story in the locker room afterward. He was spontaneous, affectionate, and loyal to his friends, all of whom called him Bob, which he preferred, although the name "Bobby" was being perpetuated by the press. Perhaps his closest friend was his father, Robert P. Jones, whom everybody called "Colonel." (Bobby was named for his paternal grandfather, Robert T. Jones, who thought golf was a waste of time.) Jones's father scored in the high 70s, and Bobby would forever remain nostalgic that he had won the championship of his home club in Atlanta, East Lake, when he was thirteen by defeating his father in the final. Colonel Jones would always remain his son's favorite partner. Jones could number his personal friends from every conceivable walk of life, from celebrities on the order of Douglas Fairbanks to straight-arrow businessmen. It would be hard to find two golfers who had less in common than Jones and Gene Sarazen, yet they kept up a lifelong correspondence.

The only quality that may have topped Jones's modesty was his thoughtfulness and integrity. On the night before his Sunday play-off with Al Espinosa for that United States Open at Winged Foot, Jones, a Protestant married to a Catholic, secretly requested officials to postpone the starting time for an hour so that Espinosa might have time to attend Mass.

At four national championships Jones called penalty strokes on himself for minor breaches of the Rules. In the 1925 Open Championship at Worcester, he insisted on penalizing himself a stroke when his ball accidentally moved slightly as the blade of his iron touched the grass. No one else possibly could have seen the ball move, not even his caddie, and officials pooh-poohed the incident. But Jones insisted. That stroke cost him the title, which he lost in a play-off with Willie Macfarlane, and eventually prevented him from becoming the only man ever to win five United States Opens. When Jones was praised for throwing the book at himself, he became indignant. "There is only one way to play the game," he said. "You might as well praise a man for not robbing a bank."

As an ultra-athlete, recognized as being better at his game than any other athlete, Jones remained unaffected at a time

when flattering headlines were being made by athletes who
had not a fraction of his talent, many of whom, if the public
had been informed by the press as well as they are today, would
have been known to be a good deal more unsavory than even
the uninhibited journalism of that period cared to report.
Perhaps no other section of American history has been more
innocently recorded than the sports scene during the Roaring
Twenties, yet Jones remained a man who was beyond the need
of publicity when all around him odd characters by the dozens
were being manufactured into public heroes. His public utter-
ances were models of restraint and decorum, and so the image
of him that was projected through the newspapers was impec-
cably true to life, not larger than it.

And project he did; there is no other way to describe the
way his personality reached out and grabbed the public of two
continents. He had that guileless look of a scoutmaster about
him, as Ouimet had, but he had turned what Ouimet had done
in golf 180 degrees. Where Ouimet had done the "impossible"
by defeating two of the finest pros in the game, Jones had
made it all but impossible for the finest pros in the game to
beat him. And Jones was no playboy, like Jerry Travers. Nor
was he outgoing, like Chick Evans. When Jones spoke, in public or in private, his thoughts were measured, his words
selected, his tone of voice modulated. He evolved as every
boy's buddy, every girl's boyfriend, every mother's and father's
son—everybody's hero in some lovingly fantasized model.

Long before he won his first championship, there had
been an enormous amount of expectation from Jones that
might have stifled the talent of any other youngster. He had
caught the public's attention beginning with his startling
debut in the 1916 Amateur. With no championships held
during the war, Jones toured much of the country playing

exhibitions for the Red Cross with an older clubmate, Perry Adair, and with two older and very pretty girls: Elaine Rosenthal, Chicago's leading amateur who had been runner-up in the 1914 Women's Amateur Championship of the United States, and, from Atlanta, Alexa Stirling, who had won that championship just before the war and who would win the two immediately after it. The scores that Jones shot during those exhibitions were soon being talked about among golfers clear to the trenches of France.

Just after the war, F. Scott Fitzgerald was busy writing his first novel, *This Side of Paradise*, back home in St. Paul, Minnesota, while carrying on a stormy, long-distance affair with a girl from Montgomery, Alabama, named Zelda Sayre, whom he had met in officer-candidate school. Impatient with Fitzgerald because he would not set a wedding date, Zelda tried to make him jealous by sending Fitzgerald a signed photograph of the most famous athlete in the South that she could think of. Although he was two years younger than she, that athlete turned out to be Bobby Jones. The picture was signed, "With love, Bobby." Evidently the ruse worked, for Fitzgerald and Zelda were married not long afterward, thus beginning one of the zaniest and most tragic marriages in American letters. Fitzgerald would never learn that the words had been forged by Zelda, nor would any of Fitzgerald's biographers, of which there were several. Indeed, Jones himself didn't learn of the forgery until forty-five years later. He thought the situation "ludicrous." Zelda Sayre had been a notorious boy-chaser and party-goer, and would become the flapper personified. "I only met her once, casually, at a party in Augusta," recalled Jones, who eight years after meeting Zelda would marry an Atlanta beauty named Mary Malone. "I assure you that eighteen-year-old girls then, as now, didn't

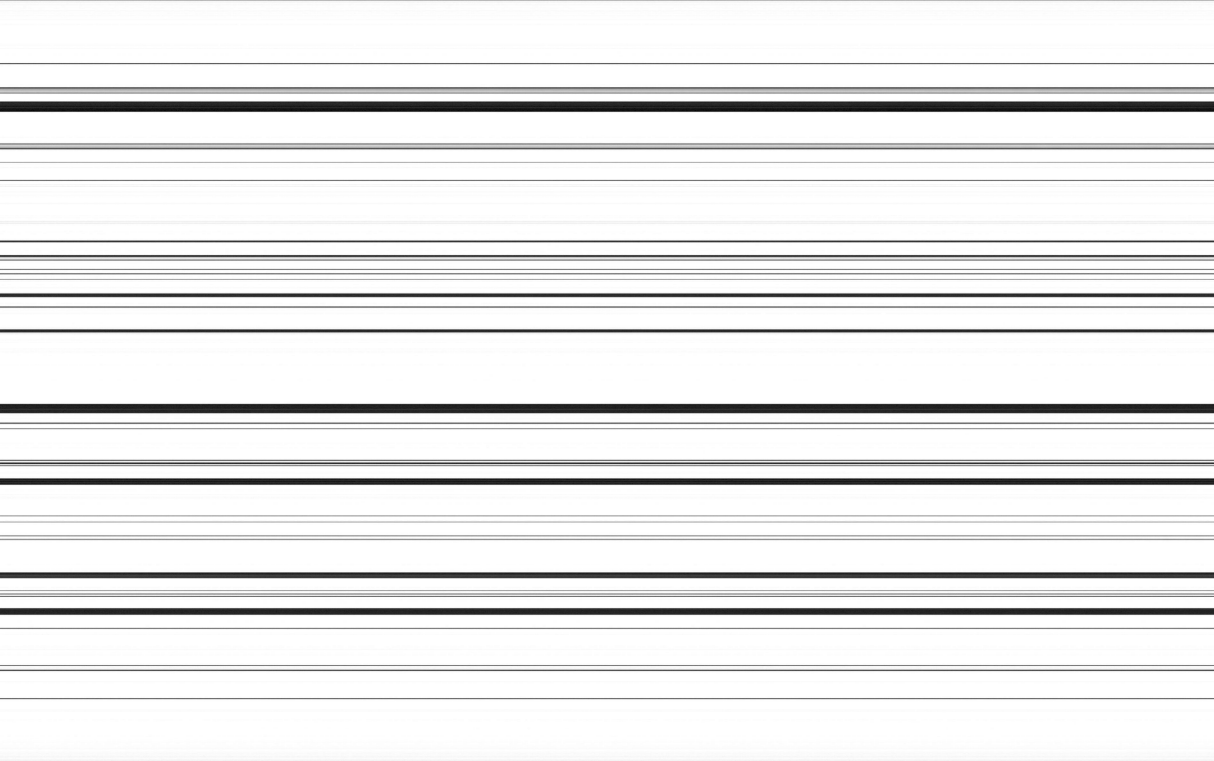

matter who
Bobby Jones

n the Open
reat Britain,
nore in golf.
unlikely age
tobiography,
Keeler, and
ortswriter in
ten stay, and
er become a
he book was
veekly maga-
printing and
in 1985 as a

pularity more
eer. In 1923,
not a million
last champi-
n three times
the game has
of that growth
ause he hadn't
played more
e Barrymores
al strongmen,
the act in cen-
apeze. Unable
though Hagen
ot enter—they

had to stand by while
on top of another for
    As far as the public
golf being played the
professional. They wer
golf everybody else pla
    With his fans—an
spectators could reach
was monumental. He
favor seekers, storyte
social opportunists, se
and other assorted pe
knew," wrote sportswr
as he saw them, "who
possible every penalty
licity in the United St
    Jones's popularity fo
golf had become but a
when Arnold Palmer,
monopolizing the game
to London after the Br
round in the suburbs, h
At Victoria Station, gol
the driver the name o
unable to miss the acce
Yank!" he asked. "Do yo

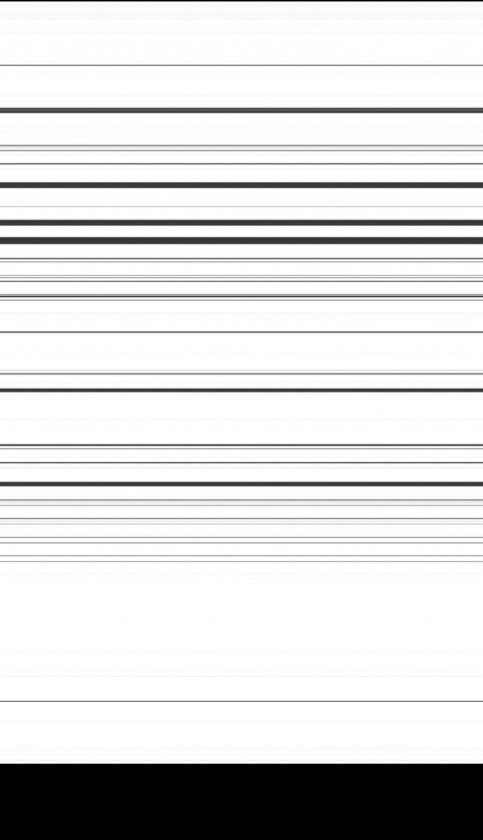

pay any attention to sixteen-year-old boys, no matter who they were." Notwithstanding, that is how famous Bobby Jones had been, even before he won a championship.

After Jones became, in 1926, the first to win the Open Championships of both the United States and Great Britain, the public could not see how he could do much more in golf. Publishers wanted a book by him. And so, at the unlikely age of twenty-four, Bobby Jones put together his autobiography, *Down the Fairway*, written with the help of O. B. Keeler, and with a foreword by Grantland Rice, the famous sportswriter in whose New York apartment young Jones would often stay, and with whose daughter, Florence (who would later become a movie star), Jones began a lifelong friendship. The book was serialized in *Liberty*, one of the nation's largest weekly magazines. Within two months, it went into a third printing and eventually into a fifth. A sixth was brought out in 1985 as a golf classic.

Nothing could take the measure of Jones's popularity more than the growth of the game parallel to his career. In 1923, when he won his first championship, there were not a million golfers in America. By the time he had won his last championship, seven years later, there were more than three times that many, the largest single period of growth the game has experienced before or since. To be sure, much of that growth had been due to Hagen and, to a lesser extent because he hadn't hit his stride, Sarazen. Between them, they played more exhibitions in the hinterlands of golf than the Barrymores did theaters. But they were golf's professional strongmen, watched mainly in sideshows. Bobby Jones was the act in center ring, the daring young man on the flying trapeze. Unable to win a championship that Jones played in—although Hagen would win three British Opens that Jones did not enter—they had to stand by while Jones made most of the headlines, one on top of another for eight straight years.

As far as the public was concerned, there were two types of golf being played then, and they were not just amateur and professional. They were the golf Bobby Jones played—and the golf everybody else played, Hagen at the head of it.

With his fans—and he played in championships when spectators could reach out and touch him—Jones's patience was monumental. He took them all in good-natured stride—favor seekers, storytellers, party crashers, name-droppers, social opportunists, self-promoters, kissin' cousins, drunks, and other assorted pests. "He was the only celebrity I ever knew," wrote sportswriter Paul Gallico, who called athletes as he saw them, "who was prepared to accept as gracefully as possible every penalty there is to be paid for fame and publicity in the United States."

Jones's popularity followed him long after his earthquake golf had become but a memory—like groundswells. In 1964, when Arnold Palmer, Gary Player, and Jack Nicklaus were monopolizing the game, an American friend of all three flew to London after the British Open at St. Andrews. Playing a round in the suburbs, he then took the train back to London. At Victoria Station, golf bag in hand, he hailed a taxi and told the driver the name of his hotel. Eyeing the golf bag and unable to miss the accent, the driver turned in his seat. "I say, Yank!" he asked. "Do you happen to know Bobby Jones?"

CHAPTER 4:
THE GRAND SLAM

B efore the competitive season in 1930 had begun, Bobby Jones had gone as far in golf as an amateur could be expected to go. Had he never won another national championship—and the ones he had won were *international*, really—his name would have remained inerasably in the record books for as long as golf would be played. But now he was ready for something else, something more. He was ready for the unapproachable, the unachievable, the unthought-of. Since golf couldn't take him any place he hadn't been, he was going to take it to outer reaches the public didn't know the game had.

Hereafter, history would have to find a new way of perceiving golfers. Bobby Jones was going into the game's fourth dimension, into time-space, into the immeasurable by see-touch standards.

There had been practical reasons for choosing 1930 to do this thing in golf for which he did not have a name and—now that he had confided in his uncle-confessor—for which O. B. Keeler didn't yet have one, either. Jones had picked 1930 to try to win all four championships because his finances and family obligations simply would not permit him to play in all of them any more. Part of the problem was solved for him by the USGA, which would pay most of his expenses abroad for the Walker Cup Match, which was to be played at Royal St. George's, Sandwich.

The match was scheduled for late May, somewhat earlier than usual. Immediately following it would be the British Amateur, the sole major title Jones had failed to capture. He thought it expedient, therefore, to whip himself and his game into shape somewhat before he normally would. That winter he reduced his weight, which had always been a minor problem, by working out on the stage of an abandoned theater in downtown Atlanta, where he played a game called "Doug," a cross between paddle tennis and badminton, which had been devised by his friend Douglas Fairbanks. Once satisfied with his physical condition, Jones then entered two tournaments that would feature most of the top professionals in the country.

The first event was the Savannah Open, which was played late in February. In the first round, Jones broke the course record with a 67. This was broken in the second round with a 66 by twenty-two-year-old Horton Smith, who had won seven tournaments and been second in four others during the winter circuit. In the third round, Jones broke Smith's record with a 65. But he eventually lost the event when he hit a shot out of bounds on the next-to-last hole. The Savannah Open was the last formal competition Jones would not win.

The second event was the Southeastern Open, in Augusta, which was played late in March. In his own opinion, this would technically be the best tournament (or nonchampionship) golf Jones ever played. When he reached the sixteenth tee of the final round, he needed three pars to win by *eighteen strokes*. A par-three, the sixteenth had created a traffic jam, and by the time Jones arrived at the tee, sixteen players were waiting to tee off. To kill time, he sat under a tree to chat with Granny Rice and Ty Cobb, who had just retired from baseball. When it

Jones and O.B. Keeler with the Grand Slam trophies. USGA.

was finally his turn to tee off, forty minutes later, Jones found that his concentration had snapped. With an insurmountable lead, he complacently finished with a double-bogey, a par-five, and another double-bogey. Still, he won by thirteen strokes. Professional Bobby Cruickshank, whom Jones had defeated in a play-off for his first United States Open, had been playing just ahead of Jones. He shook his head in amazement at the way Jones had toyed with the field. "Bob is just too good," he remarked to O. B. Keeler, prophetically. "He's going to win the British Amateur and the British Open and then he's coming back here to win the National Open and the National Amateur. They'll never stop him *this* year."

Jones, his wife, Keeler, and a rooting section of Atlanta golfers sailed for England in late April aboard the *Mauretania*.

Among the other passengers were Douglas Fairbanks, Maurice Chevalier, Sir Joseph Duveen, the art connoisseur, and Harry Lauder, the music-hall entertainer. Fairbanks planned to watch the Walker Cup Match, but pressing business back in the United States would prevent him from watching the Amateur Championship. He promised to return on the next ship for the British Open. The man who made a living rescuing distressed maidens from twenty-foot balconies was that thrilled at the prospect of watching Bobby Jones play in a golf championship.

In the foursome matches at Sandwich, Jones, as captain of the team, paired himself with Doc Willing, who had been runner-up at Pebble Beach the year before and was conceded to be the most erratic member of the squad. Playing in the number-two position, they won their match eight and seven. With characteristic modesty, Jones dropped himself into second position for the singles so that Jimmy Johnston, as Amateur champion, might have the honor of playing first. Jones won his match against Roger Wethered nine and eight.

Between the Walker Cup Match and the British Amateur at St. Andrews, most of the members of both teams took a day off to play in a thirty-six-hole tournament sponsored by *Golf Illustrated*. Jones won it by a stroke. Now he was ready for the British Amateur—the first vector on what would later be called the "impregnable quadrilateral."

As it is with a lot of stupendous things, the most difficult part of the Grand Slam was getting it off the ground. The British Amateur proved to be the most obstinate championship of Jones's life. Before it was over, he managed to extract from it the last possible ounce of drama. Keeler would call it "destiny." Jones would call it "luck."

In the very first round, Jones was drawn against an utterly unknown player, named Sid Roper, from the Robin Hood district of Nottingham, who, figuratively, came close to robbing Jones of the Grand Slam. As was his invariable habit, Jones approached Roper on the first tee, looked squarely into his eyes, and then offered that smile that had "good luck" written all over it. Long afterward, Jones would distinctly remember that Roper looked unmistakably like a man who would play his best golf under pressure.

Jones opened up with a barrage that surprised even him and that left his sophisticated St. Andrews gallery bug-eyed. He made a birdie-three, a par-four, a birdie-three, an eagle-two, and a birdie-three. Five under par for five holes, he still had Roper only three down. Furthermore, Roper showed no signs of being the least bit concerned. He picked up a hole by laying Jones a stymie on the eighth, and then matched him stroke for stroke until he ran out of holes on the sixteenth green. And that was the match: Jones, three and two.

Jones's closest match came against Cyril Tolley, the defending champion, in the fourth round. The wind was blowing at such a force off the River Eden that it tore the sand out of the bunkers and turned the Old Course's outsized greens into skating rinks. Still, every man, woman, and child in town came out to see the match. (Later, a playwright would write a mystery based on the altogether plausible fact that the Jones-Tolley match was the perfect occasion for someone to rob a local bank, since the streets would be empty. The play is still performed at times when the British Open is played at St. Andrews.)

Jones and Tolley had each been one up three different times by the time they finished the sixteenth hole. The seventeenth hole on the Old Course is one of the most famous in all golf, and one of the oddest. For those who are less than very long off the tee, the drive must be played to the left of a building that stands directly in line with the green, 466 yards away. The building is today the Old Course Golf and Country Club, but then it was known as "Auchterlonie's drying sheds," a barnlike structure where Laurie Auchterlonie, a famous clubmaker/ professional who won the United States Open in 1902, had stored hickory shafts till the sap dried out of them. (A namesake nephew who became a distinguished clubmaker would many years later become honorary professional at the R & A.)

For golfers who had the length of Jones and Tolley, though, the drive called to be hit over the sheds, where it would fly well past Cheape's Bunker on the left but still stay way short of the Scholar's Bunker, which encroaches from the left rough practically to midfairway and comes into play only for ordinary golfers. Because most of them had to drive to the left of the drying sheds, making the hole much longer than it says on the scorecard, Americans regarded the hole as playing to a par of five, the Scots then having ignored par, preferring instead to keep score by playing to "level fours."

With the wind at their backs, Jones's drive was slightly to the left of Tolley's and slightly shorter. The flagstick was placed in its most strategic position, directly behind a pot bunker that guards the left-front of the green, the right-rear of which is skirted by a road, behind which is a stone wall, both of which are played as hazards. To make matters even more ticklish, the green, the road, and the wall are all situated on the bias, slanting 45 degrees toward the player from left to right.

Surveying the situation, Jones took much more time than usual. He did not relish playing downwind out of that pot bunker, and he had to avoid both the road and the wall at any cost. He elected to play his second shot in a way he had never seen or heard of before—to the upper part of the green and toward the eighteenth tee. He asked the stewards to move back the gallery, and joined in waving them back himself.

Playing his mashie-iron, a four-iron, he hit the shot precisely as he had planned, only to have it hit a bewildered spectator. But the ball came to rest almost exactly where he had hoped.

Tolley played to the right of the bunker, toward the broad expanse of green that lay below the cup. But he didn't quite catch the ball cleanly and it stopped just short of the pot bunker. He then played an exquisite pitch two feet from the hole, a shot that years later he declared was the finest of his career. Jones sank an eight-footer after his approach and, after Tolley holed his putt, they marched to the eighteenth, all even.

Still playing downwind, both Jones and Tolley left their drives only thirty feet short of the green, 354 yards away, Jones more to the left, from where he played a pitch-and-run through the Valley of Sin, a huge swale that stood between him and the flagstick. He left his ball twenty-five feet past the hole. Tolley, playing a standard pitch, lay half that distance. Both missed, and so they went to the first tee for extra holes.

After both hit good drives against the wind, Jones bore an iron through it, twelve feet from the hole. Tolley hit a slack second that left him a light pitch, which he stopped seven feet from the cup. The only mistake Jones could then make would be to three-putt. He lagged his putt, as he always did, to within inches of the cup—and laid Tolley a stymie that couldn't possibly be negotiated. And that was the match. Jones was so exhausted by the desperate urgency of the struggle that he felt as though he had fought a battle "with broadswords."

Jones was not forced to undergo the ordeal of any more extra-hole matches, but he had his anxious moments, all of them against Jimmy Johnston and George Voigt, whose match against one another Jones had refereed at Pebble Beach the year before. With five holes to play in the fifth round against Johnston, Jones found himself four up. But then, in quick order, Johnston won the fourteenth with a birdie, Jones messed up the fifteenth to lose it to a par, they halved the sixteenth, and Johnston won the seventeenth with a birdie. Going to the eighteenth one up, Jones had the eerie feeling that, come what may, he could not lose this championship. Faced with an eight-footer on the last green for a halve and the match, he knew before he stroked the putt that it could not stay out. And it didn't.

In an afternoon match the next day against Voigt, Jones—after unwisely sipping a glass of sherry during lunch that had thrown off his depth perception—found himself two down with five holes to play. With the huge gallery standing almost on top of them, Voigt apparently did not realize the strength of the wind blowing from his left off St. Andrews Bay. He did not aim safely enough into the vast Elysian Fields, as the fourteenth fairway is called, and then watched haplessly as his drive floated out of bounds to the right. Jones won the sixteenth when Voigt bunkered his drive. And so they were all even playing seventeen, where Jones found himself facing a twelve-foot putt for a half. Once again, he had that feeling of predestination. Although the putt had a curl to it, the line looked as obvious as a rainspout. The putt dropped, just as Jones knew it would, and he won the eighteenth hole from a shattered Voigt with ease.

In the final, Jones played against Roger Wethered, brother of Britain's great woman amateur, Joyce. Although Wethered had won this championship back in 1923, and had been runner-up in 1928, he was no match against someone as determined as Jones, especially over thirty-six holes and at St. Andrews, a course Jones could handle the way Shakespeare might a crossword puzzle. Since no amateur in the world stood better than an even-money chance to take Jones past the thirtieth hole, that turned out to be where the match ended. Fifteen thousand spectators then swamped Jones in an effort "to see what made him tick," as Keeler would write, describing their enthusiasm. Jones had to be escorted by the local constabulary clear to the clubhouse of the Royal and Ancient, a mile and a half away. A band had been set to play him in, but it never sounded a note, so complete was the pandemonium.

After the British Amateur, Jones spent a week with Mary relaxing in Paris, where he won an informal four-ball match with Jimmy Johnston against France's leading amateur and professional. Then he went to Hoylake for the British Open, where he played the sloppiest golf of the Grand Slam. On one hole he took a seven after being hole-high in two, and yet he managed to lead the field all the way, breaking the seventy-two-hole course record by a clean ten strokes. It was clear that

Mary and Bobby Jones aboard ship after returning from a British Open triumph. Bettman.

if anybody was going to stop Jones from winning a championship that year, it was not going to be Jones himself

The sixteenth hole at Hoylake is 532 yards long. Two hundred seventy yards from the tee is a dike, around which the fairway bends to form a sharp dogleg to the right. The green is wide and flat, and to the left of it is a yawning bunker. After a tremendous drive in the last round, Jones hit a towering brassie, or two-wood, that pulled just enough to land in the bunker. When he examined his ball, he found it to be lying on the sand so close to the far bank of the bunker that he would not be able to make a normal backswing. Desperately in need of a birdie at this point, since everybody was playing well, Jones elected to play the shot with a concave niblick, or nine-iron, to the back of which had been added twenty-five ounces of lead, giving it the feel of a sledgehammer. It was the forerunner of the sand wedge, and had been given to him by Horton Smith earlier in the year at the Savannah Open. Jones had hit only two shots with it before, both of them unimportant. He addressed the ball with his right foot resting on top of the bank, and then hit the ball with a sharp, descending blow. A teaspoonful of sand too much, and Jones would have left the ball in the bunker. A teaspoonful too little, and he would have sent it skidding across the green. The ball popped over the front bank of the bunker, crept across the green, and then trickled two inches past the cup. Jones finished with two more fours on the next two holes, back-breakers both, and became the first man to equal John Ball's feat of winning both the Open and Amateur Championships of Great Britain in the same season, a record that had stood for forty years.

On his return to New York City aboard the SS *Europa*, Jones was given another ticker-tape parade up Broadway from The Bowery to City Hall, while the band played "Valencia." It was the same traditional parade used to honor Gen. John J.

Pershing after the First World War and to honor Charles Lindbergh for flying the Atlantic solo, and it would be the same to honor Gen. Dwight D. Eisenhower after the Second World War and to honor astronaut John Glenn. Jones remains the only person to have been so honored *twice*.

A rooting section of 250 fans from Atlanta had taken a special train to New York to welcome their hero home. Many of them would go on to Minneapolis for the United States Open with Jones aboard the Twentieth Century Limited.

At Interlachen, Jones found himself in the middle of one of the worst heat waves Minneapolis had ever endured. Temperatures were over 100 degrees and the humidity was almost as high. To make matters more formidable, Interlachen, with its abundance of lakes and its smallish greens, had allowed the rough to grow knee-high. Jones shot a two-under 70 while other members of the field held umbrellas against the sun, wore wide-brimmed hats, and dabbed their foreheads with ice packs. Several contestants experienced dizzy spells; one of them fainted. Jones was so soaked with perspiration that the Reddy Tees in the pocket of his knickers stained through. A foulard necktie dyed his broadcloth shirt red and could not be untied. Keeler cut it off with a penknife.

Jones won this, the third vector of the "impregnable quadrilateral," by the simple expedient of becoming the first man in the history of the Open to break par for seventy-two holes. In the third round, he spun off seven birdies in the first sixteen holes, three of them by knocking his second shots inches from the flagstick. He might have waltzed away with the championship if an incident had not occurred in the last round that can only be described as bizarre.

The seventeenth hole at Interlachen was the longest par-three in Open history, 263 yards to a green bordered by bunkers. (It was birdied only once, by Hagen.) After getting a birdie on sixteen, Jones pushed his brassie shot to seventeen wildly. There were fifteen thousand spectators at Interlachen that day, three-quarters of whom were fighting to see Jones, if only for a glimpse of him. None of them saw where Jones's ball bounced. Some thought it had ricocheted into a lake, but couldn't swear it had. Wherever it bounced, it was never found, although two hundred people looked for five minutes.

His chin like granite, Jones dropped another ball and made a double-bogey, what with the stroke-and-distance penalty. At eighteen, he underestimated the club he had needed to reach the flagstick at the back of the green, and left himself with a forty-foot putt up a bank and the very real possibility of three-putting to go into a play-off. He stroked the putt in his usual molasses style. While it was still rolling, ten feet from the hole, he started walking toward it. He knew it was in. And it was.

There was no waving of a cap, no shaking of a fist in the air. Jones simply smiled bashfully. This was not a man beating incalculable odds, showing how good he might be, realizing how lucky he could get. This was a man walking toward an unnamed destiny, nonchalantly because he knew it was preordained.

All Jones had to do now to accomplish what would be called the Grand Slam, in the opinion of golfers everywhere, was to keep breathing until September for the United States Amateur at Merion, the same course where he had made his golf debut fourteen years before as a boy. Curiously, the wait turned out to be not without hazards of its own. One afternoon that summer, while playing a friendly round at East Lake, Jones was caught in a violent thunderstorm during which lightning bolts narrowly missed him as he ran for the clubhouse. One bolt exploded a double-chimney of the clubhouse as Jones was passing underneath it, blasting bricks and mortar three hundred feet away, the debris from which tore the shirt off Jones's back and left a six-inch gash on his shoulder. Not three weeks later, Jones was walking along a deserted sidewalk in downtown Atlanta on his way to a luncheon engagement when a runaway car mounted the curb and crashed into the very spot from which he had made a split-second broad jump. Only days before the championship, he had unthinkingly tried to catch a blade in midair that had slipped from his razor. Luckily, he only scratched his hand.

Once at Merion, Jones, unmindful of his opponents, savaged the golf course. He won the medal with a 69 and a 73, equaling the thirty-six-hole record for the course. From then on, he was never down to an opponent and never in any sort of trouble. He won both his eighteen-hole matches five and four. In the thirty-six-hole matches that he preferred, he won six and five, nine and eight, and, in the final against a hapless Gene Homans, eight and seven. On that eleventh green, Homans had an eighteen-foot putt to keep the match alive. Before it had stopped rolling, he held out his hand to Jones with a big smile.

By shaking Jones's hand, Homans had thereby conceded the ten-inch putt Jones had left on the eleventh green, which sits in a nook across a babbling brook in a cathedral of trees. There was a moment of eerie, churchlike silence. Then pandemonium once again broke loose. The gallery was the largest in the USGA's history—eighteen thousand—certainly a record anywhere for a single match. Everyone in it, it seemed, clapped, howled, shrieked, and roared at once. The clubhouse was six hundred yards away, and it would take a cordon of fifty marines to get Jones there unhurt by a delirious crowd that wanted to shake his hand or simply to touch him, just to see if he was real. "It was," said the *New York Times* of those six hundred yards, "the most triumphant journey that any man ever traveled in sport."

In Merion's smallish clubhouse—despite Prohibition still in legal but not realistic force—champagne, corn whiskey, or bathtub gin was in everybody's hands. Jones's father, the colonel, was lost in the crowd, yelling, "Where's my boy? Where's my boy?" Mary Jones had stayed home in Atlanta to care for their two youngsters, Clara and young Bob. She was told the news over the phone by a reporter for the *Atlanta Journal*. "That's grand," she said in the background voice she reserved for her husband's golf. "It's a comfort to know it's all over."

For a caddie, Jones had drawn from the pool a nineteen-year-old named Howard Rexford. He waited in a corridor of the clubhouse, his whole body wrapped protectively around Jones's bag of clubs. Howard refused to allow anybody to so much as look at them until Jones came out of the locker room. Although Jones had never asked him for any advice, young Howard had been touched with how thoughtful Jones had been toward him. Finally, Jones stepped out of the locker room to fetch his clubs. He reached out to shake Howard's hand and thanked him, as though he could not possibly have won the championship without his aid, Rexford would recall. The youngster could feel some bills in Jones's hand. Without looking at them, he stuffed them in his shoe, walked to the eighteenth fairway that Jones and he had never come close to during the five matches, and then took off on a run through the woods that skirt the left-hand side of the fairway. When he ran out of breath, he sat down and removed his shoe. There were ten twenty-dollar bills folded over, five times more than he had ever earned in one week. Overcome by Jones's generosity and overwrought by the history he had been party to, he began to sob.

Immediately after the Amateur Championship, public reaction was not to the Grand Slam itself, which some newspapers didn't even capitalize if they mentioned it at all, but just to that championship, as though it were hardly more than what was to be expected, now that Jones had also won the three other major championships that season. There was little of the bombast over a Grand Slam that might have been expected, looking back today. Coming one atop another, the four championships of 1930 had caused a mass myopia with the other championships that had preceded them, leaving the public too dazzled to separate the four championships of the Grand Slam from Jones's total of thirteen. There was a vacuum of superlatives among the press; as though unable to find ones purple enough, it didn't use any. For even the most experienced golfers, let alone a press that, until Jones, had regarded golf as a secondary sport, didn't know quite how to bring those four championships of one season into focus. That would take time—years, in fact.

Philadelphia's newspapers had assigned dozens of reporters to cover Jones at Merion, some of whom had never been on a golf course before. (Among the more knowledgeable was a young sportswriter named Joseph C. Dey, Jr., later to become executive secretary of the USGA and much more in golf, whose assignment was to report every shot Jones played.) But the day after the championship, the *Philadelphia Inquirer*, to illustrate how astigmatic the public was toward the Grand Slam, devoted only a single but long column to what Jones had done at Merion. There was no mention of any "Grand Slam," only that Jones had won his fourth championship of the season and had expressed vague plans for his future afterward. Even in dispatches back to the *Atlanta Journal*, O. B. Keeler wrote little or nothing about a "Grand Slam." He followed this story up with an article for *The American Golfer*, and still did not use the expression "Grand Slam."

The term would become part of golf's history very slowly. Fourteen years after the Grand Slam, the Associated Press would vote it the all-time achievement in sports. Eighteen years after, a young editor for *The New Yorker*, named Herbert Warren Wind, would write *The Story of American Golf* one of the most intelligent, perhaps the most literate, and certainly the best-documented history written on any sport. In it, he said that the Grand Slam could never be surpassed and would be equaled about the time men are pole-vaulting twenty feet and women are running the four-minute mile." The statement was not hyperbolic. If anything, it stands today as an understatement.

The public could not immediately grasp what Jones had done because the Grand Slam was something ethereal. It was absolute golf: stroke and match, amateur and open, lucky bounces and, yet, not without its rubs of the green. There had been no precedent they could touch, and nothing to surpass it they could see.

Jones had had a love for serious music since, at thirteen, his mother, Clara Jones, had dragged him to a performance of the Metropolitan Opera on tour in Atlanta. From then on, his head was full of arias by Wagner, Verdi, Puccini. Once he got to understand serious music, he would hear the anecdote about a young girl listening to Beethoven's Ninth Symphony for the first time. Transfixed by the ominous moans of the opening movement, she sat in silence through the electric second movement and its pastoral interludes, through the soaring melody of the third, and finally through the Ode to Joy in the fourth and last movement, with its four soloists and choir of a hundred voices. For a little while, Beethoven had made time stand still for her. Too enraptured to clap her hands, she turned to her parents after the applause had died down. "What must we do now?" she said.

That's how the world of golf felt about the Grand Slam. "What must we do now?" it asked. And nobody had an answer.

CHAPTER 5:
IN RETIREMENT

Sometime during the 1930 championship campaign, Jones had told O. B. Keeler of his plans to retire, probably while they were returning aboard the *Europa* from the British Open. He asked Keeler to keep the news a secret. He did not want to put added pressure on himself in the United States championships or put undue emphasis on them in the newspapers.

But in a locker-room interview after the Open Championship at Interlachen, Jones had been baited by a reporter unwittingly. "What are you going to do when you retire?" the reporter asked. The question was more facetious than serious.

Jones grinned, took a sip from the corn whiskey in his hand, and nodded toward Keeler, who had just stepped out of a shower, a towel wrapped around his waist. "You'd better tell them, O. B. You know." Jones knew that Keeler also knew *not* to tell them anything specific.

Keeler was a man even more widely read than Jones. For one thing, he could read Greek and Latin. He was fond of reciting poetry, and he could do so entertainingly by the hour, interspersing Ovid, for example, with hundreds of bawdy limericks.

Taking Jones's cue, Keeler climbed on top of a bench, drink in hand, and began to recite from Hilaire Belloc, the English poet who had been born in France:

> If ever I become a rich man
> Or if ever I grow to be old,
> I will build a house with a deep thatch
> To shelter me from the cold,
> I will hold my house in the high woods
> Within a walk of the sea,
> And the men that were boys when I was a boy
> Shall sit and drink with me.

The verse had just enough of a hint to let the public know that Jones had some degree of retirement in the recesses of his mind, but it was vague enough not to let anybody know what it was. In truth, Jones himself wasn't altogether sure how that retirement would work out, either. But everybody knew he just wasn't going to sit back and talk over old times with his friends.

After winning the Amateur Championship at Merion, Jones had been pressured further about his future plans. But those plans still weren't cut and dried in his own mind. Retire, yes. But how? And to what degree? After all, he was only twenty-eight. But, after all, fifteen of those years had not been so tender, having been spent playing competitive golf, almost all of it championship golf and almost all of that *national* championship golf.

At a formal ceremony by the USGA on the veranda at Merion that overlooks the first tee, Jones was for the fifth time awarded the Havemeyer Trophy, emblematic of the Amateur Championship and named after Theodore Havemeyer, the first president of the USGA. Jones felt obliged to make some sort of public statement, however gauzy.

"I expect to continue to play golf," he said almost offhandedly in his slight Georgian drawl, "but just when and where I cannot say now. I have no definite plans either to retire or as to when and where I may continue in competition. I might play next year and lay off in 1932. I might stay out next season and feel like another tournament the following year. What I want most right now is to be free of any obligation, express or implied, to continue playing each year in both major championships."

What was couched in the statement was that Jones might feel like playing in another "tournament." But, then, he seldom played in mere tournaments anyhow, having played in only seven during the past eight years. What he was really saying, in a manner that would not offend the USGA, of whose executive committee he was then a member, was that he did not want to be obligated to play in its championships, of which he had become conjointly the star attraction and its biggest source of revenue.

At Merion, he had been begged by officials to play an extra practice round the day before the championship itself began. Ordinarily, Jones liked to take this day off from golf and rest, maybe going fishing or just sitting around his hotel room reading a book. (One example was the critically acclaimed *Life of Christ* by Giovanni Papini, who, prophetically, had converted to Catholicism, as would Jones late in life.) But now that the Depression was being felt throughout the country, the USGA was in sore need of funds. At Merion, thanks almost entirely to Jones's presence, the gate receipts had been more than $55,000. Thirty-five years later, inflation and all, they wouldn't be a third that. When the first United States

Open without Jones in twelve years was played in 1931, receipts fell off more than 50 percent.

After the Amateur Championship, Jones went home to Atlanta to think of his retirement plans in the concrete. Keeler had coined "Grand Slam," and the four championships together were now being called just that throughout the country. George Trevor, of the *New York Sun*, had first described the four titles as the "impregnable quadrilateral," which didn't fit the national vernacular as well as Keeler's phrase and was, besides, too long for a headline.

Whatever it was being called, the dimensions of it began to take shape in Jones's mind. He felt that its importance was not so much "a monument to skill in playing the game." To him, its importance lay far beyond that—"in the abstract." In short, without putting it into words, he knew that he had somehow gone into the game's fourth dimension. Whatever the name for it should be, it could not be measured in terms of the times it was made in, or within the space of his career. It was a thing apart.

Certainly, he could win another championship, after which he could only be expected to win another, and then still another. There would be no end to those expectations, all of which could only serve to diminish the Grand Slam, as now he himself began to call it.

From his readings, Jones had recollections of an Oriental school of philosophy that held that the aim of life should be the perfection of personality or character regardless of its sufferings, joys, and achievements. He also recalled that in Oriental art, a single flower is regarded as having more inherent beauty than a whole bouquet. Jones did not see how he could improve upon his character any more through championship golf, nor improve upon the Grand Slam by embellishing it with a bouquet of half a dozen more national titles. (Or, more likely, a dozen.) Besides, he had more practical matters to attend to: a family with eventually three children to support, a law practice to pursue, dozens of business opportunities to take advantage of.

Six weeks later, on November 18, Jones sent a dry, unsentimental statement to the USGA—free of any rhetorical loopholes—formally announcing his complete retirement from championship golf, adding that he was surrendering his amateur status to embark on some golf enterprises that would earn him some much-needed money.

The USGA immediately released the statement to the press. Although it was the height of the football season, the news made banner headlines in most of the country's major newspapers and a lot of those in the British Isles, mainly on the front pages. *The New York Times* ran an unprecedented editorial. "With dignity," it said, ending in blank verse, "he quits the memorable scene on which he nothing common did, or mean."

The news shocked those golfers who presumed that, since Jones was no longer an amateur, he would play golf for money. But he had nothing of the kind in mind, although he might have made a tidy fortune just playing exhibitions. Actually, he placed himself in a position no other golfer before or since had: a state of limbo between amateurism and professionalism. He was simply a former amateur who had decided never to play golf for money. Then he settled down to the business of being a gentleman lawyer in the South, where his name had begun to be spoken with a reverence theretofore reserved for Robert E. Lee and Eli Whitney.

Jones chose those enterprises that he thought tastefully reflected his career, rather than indiscriminately endorsing every hair tonic and shoe polish, every gadget and gimmick

that was tossed on his desk, and he undertook only those ven-
tures that required more active participation than the mere
affixing of his signature. For the new talking pictures, he made
a series of one-reel instructional films that rank even today as
the most lucid of their type ever filmed, although he disliked
the "corny" but necessary story lines that were written into
them. These transparent plots had him giving tips to movie
stars, all of whom, unknown to the public, worked without pay

On location filming instructional "shorts" for Warner Brothers. Bettman.

just to get a free lesson from "the Emperor Jones," as he had been called during the height of his career, a title sportswriters picked up from the 1920 play of the same name by Eugene O'Neill. The "guest stars" were used to grab the attention of the vast theater audiences who had never played golf and probably never would. It was estimated that the films, eighteen in all, were seen by twenty-five million people. Jones actually had become the movie star everybody said he looked like.

Jones also kept up his newspaper column, and turned out occasional articles for Granny Rice's *American Golfer*, the slick Condé Nast monthly that was now carrying such major bylines as Ring Lardner and Clarence Budington Kelland, in addition to every well-known sportswriter and famous golfer in the world. He narrated another instructional series for national radio, which was then as carefully produced an entertainment medium as current-day television.

Through nobody's fault, and certainly not his own, it was the one venture Jones would come to regret. Radio just couldn't lend itself to golf. Millions of people who had never seen Jones play nevertheless knew his face and figure from newspapers and magazines. But without being able actually to see him swing a golf club, they couldn't fully appreciate him. As Bernard Darwin had written, that swing had a touch of poetry. And that poetry, as poetry has a way of doing, came across even to those who did not altogether capture the sense of it.

Jones's chief undertaking was with A. G. Spalding & Bros., for whom he helped design a set of woods and irons, calling on his mechanical-engineering skills. Until then, all mass-produced irons in America had possessed long, thin, tinny blades that gave a shot an unpleasantly brittle feel. What Jones was after was a sensation approximating the powerful squash that you could get from Scottish clubs, particularly the irons hand-hewn and cast by master-club-maker Tom Stewart, which he and practically every other front-rank American golfer imported. After overseeing the casting of the irons and sanding the shafts by hand himself back in Atlanta, Jones had rejected more than two hundred different clubs until he arrived at the set that satisfied him.

There were fifteen in all, not counting the "sand iron" he had used that one and only time at Hoylake. (The USGA limit of fourteen clubs would not be put into effect until 1938, when Joe Dey was that body's executive secretary.) Jones used four woods, ten irons, and a feather-light putter that the public called "Calamity Jane" (but which he modestly didn't), after the sharpshooting lady of the Old West. He also had a pet name for his driver, which he had personally designed while at Harvard. He called it "Jeanie Deans," after the plain but loyal heroine in Sir Walter Scott's *The Heart of Midlothian*.

Using these clubs as a prototype, Jones, with the help of Spalding's craftsmen, tried to duplicate the feel of the hand-made Scottish clubs by enlarging the sweet spot in the new clubs, or, rather, giving that area that was not in the sweet spot a solidity that would avoid making a mishit shot feel as though it had been executed with a stone. This they did by making the blades thicker and more compact and by providing a flanged sole.

The first set appeared in 1932. To accelerate production, the clubs were outfitted with steel shafts, which, near the end of Jones's career, had begun to make such in-roads on hickory that it had become obvious that they would soon supersede it as surely as the rubber-wound ball had superseded the gutta-percha. They were also numbered, thereby doing away with the old Scottish names for clubs—mid-iron, mashie, mashie-niblick, and so on—that a lot of clubmakers couldn't agree on, anyway.

The clubs were enthusiastically accepted by the public and, as a result, widely imitated by Spalding competitors. The Spalding clubs carried the Jones autograph, "Robt. T. Jones, Jr." They sold steadily for forty-one years, two years past his death.

Revisionists—those who would rewrite history through hindsight—always had a way of thinking Bobby Jones wasn't altogether real, as though he were too good a person to be true. They would argue that, while he played as an amateur, he knew there was a professional pot of gold at the end of that rainbow. This is to ignore the calendar. By the time sound had been added to motion pictures, Jones had won half his championships and almost all of them by the time "talkies" had been introduced to America's theaters. Steel shafts had made no major inroads in golf equipment; indeed, it was Jones's autographed clubs that helped popularize them. Previous to 1930, radio had been more an instrument of communication than entertainment. And Jones already had the USGA's permission to write for money. Most of these revisionists were the same people who claimed that Jones had been given preferred starting times in USGA championships, ignoring the fact that his record in Britain was better than that in the United States, not to mention the fact that Jones was the golfer most spectators wanted most to see and that he was more often than not leading the championship, anyway.

Although he was licensed to practice law without having a degree in it, Jones had no heart for the adversarial nature of the courtroom. (In law as in golf, he liked to play against the course, not the opponent.) Surely it wasn't because he had no flare for the courtroom. The day after he was admitted to practice in United States courts—in May of 1929—he won his first federal case. For the most part, though, he concentrated on business contracts with his father's firm of Jones, Evins,

Moore, and Powers, this without drawing a salary, although he was entitled to one, because so much of his time was being taken up with outside business matters.

One of the concerns the firm represented was the fast-growing Coca-Cola Company. Surprisingly, Jones made nowhere near as much money from this contact as he should have, although he was a friend of its dynamic chairman, Robert W. Woodruff, with whom he often played golf. Jones had a financial interest in bottling plants in Massachusetts, Wisconsin, Scotland, Uruguay, Argentina, and eventually Chile. But what profits the businesses showed while Jones had an interest in them were plowed back into the plants, and Jones would make no money from them until he eventually sold his interests.

In the wake of the Grand Slam, the project in which he had the most interest—what amounted to a personal passion—was the one that held the least financial promise. That was the private golf club for which he still had no site, no members, and no name. He was trying to glue together a club unique in the history of American golf, at a period in that history when literally a golf club a week would go bankrupt.

CHAPTER 6:
AUGUSTA NATIONAL

In 1857, a Belgian baron named Louis Mathieu Edouard Berckmans, who was an amateur horticulturist, purchased nearly four hundred acres on the western border of Augusta, Georgia, that had once been an indigo plantation, indigo having been one of the South's chief exports, along with cotton and rice, until the Civil War. The plantation was said to have been the site where General James Edward Oglethorpe had sat about a cheery fire of pine knots and smoked the pipe of peace with the Cherokee Indians, thereby opening the way for Georgia to become a colony and, eventually, a state.

Berckmans's son, Prosper Julius Alphonse, was also a horticulturist, and a professional one at that, as well as an agronomist. Forming a partnership under the trade name of Fruitlands Nurseries, the two Berckmanses started what may have been the first commercial nursery in the South. It was certainly the largest. A catalog they issued a few years after opening the nursery listed thirteen hundred varieties of pear and nine hundred varieties of apple. Additionally, they imported a number of trees and plants from all over the world, the progeny of which, nurtured at Fruitlands, ended up decorating the exterior of some of the South's grandest homes and

Augusta National as it looked before its course was built. Historic Golf Photos.

plantations for the next half century. Chief among their decorative plants was the azalea, which Prosper Berckmans popularized and which remains to this day the floral signature of everything below Mason and Dixon's Line.

Fruitlands Nurseries lay on the south side of what is now known as Washington Road in an area just beyond the city limits of Augusta. Baron Berckmans died in 1883, and not long afterward Prosper Berckmans lost his wife, who had borne him three sons, two of whom became horticulturists in their own rights.

In time, Prosper remarried, on this occasion to a woman thirty years younger than he. They lived together in Prosper's home, a beautiful manor house entered from Washington

Road along a carriage path, three hundred yards long, lined on both sides in sentry straightness by magnolias.

The Manor, as Prosper called the house simply enough, was not old by Augusta standards, having been built in 1854, when the property had still been an indigo plantation. But it had a degree of fame in the area for the stately simplicity of its architecture and the historical significance of having been the first house in the South to have been constructed of "artificial rock," meaning a combination of lime, gravel, and sand, or what would become known as concrete.

When Prosper died in 1910, he left the northern half of the property, which contained the manor house, to his wife, and the more developed nursery side to his sons. Only an historical guess can be made, but it would seem that the sons and their father's young widow did not see eye to eye on operating a nursery. The trade name was sold, the widow sold her half of the property, and then the sons sold their half and moved away from Augusta. One of them, Louis Alphonse, would become a successful landscape architect. Among his other achievements, he would eventually have a hand in the tastefully unobtrusive landscaping in New York City for Rockefeller Center.

During September of 1925, Augusta was visited by one of those financial figures who came out of nowhere around that time with the objective of making fast fortunes in Florida real estate. His name was Commodore J. Perry Stoltz, and he owned a hotel on Miami Beach called the Fleetwood, after a given name long in use in his wife's family. Fifteen stories tall, with a huge radio transmitter and tower on top of it, the Fleetwood Hotel was one of the grandest on Miami Beach, and perhaps its most famous. It also seems to be the only thing Stoltz was ever the commodore of.

Stoltz was visiting Augusta to look for a possible site for another Fleetwood Hotel, the second in a chain he planned to build, others to be in Chattanooga, Tennessee; Hendersonville, North Carolina; and places yet unnamed. On the basis of these plans, Stoltz was looked upon by the public much as Conrad Hilton would be years later, with a reputation that had been enhanced considerably when the city of Chattanooga was congratulated in a long, laudatory telegram by Adolph S. Ochs, owner of *The New York Times*, in securing such a "distinguished hotel man as the owner of the Fleetwood chain"—except that there was no chain as yet. The telegram was reprinted in the *Chattanooga Times*. Adolph Ochs owned it, also.

Commodore Stoltz's visit was headlined across all eight columns of the *Augusta Chronicle*, an otherwise conservative newspaper that had been publishing since 1785, making it the oldest in the South. A city historian claimed the headlines were "larger than any President received." Augusta, like most of the country elsewhere, was in the middle of a land boom.

On October 1, the *Chronicle* headlined that Commodore Stoltz would build his "Fleetwood of Augusta" on the Berckmans tract on Washington Road—the old Fruitlands Nurseries. The hotel, like the one on Miami Beach, would be fifteen stories tall, topped off by a hundred-foot radio tower. It would cost $2,000,000, an eye-popping sum in 1925. The Commodore predicted that Augusta would become a major stopover for people on their way to Miami from either New York or Chicago by the airplanes of the future. Real estate along Washington Road was quickly bought by the hundreds of acres, an estimated $3,000,000 worth in three weeks.

On January 24 of the following year, the Commodore visited Augusta again, making more headlines, to announce that his chief engineer was drawing up plans for the Augusta Fleetwood, as it would be called, which would include an eighteen-hole golf course to be designed and constructed by the same man who was to construct his hotel—which gives some idea of how much the Commodore knew about golf. At the same time, he announced plans for another Fleetwood to be built in Daytona Beach, Florida. Real estate in Augusta was really booming now. One developer announced grandiose plans for still another hotel and golf course in the town.

On February 11, the Commodore officially broke ground for the Augusta Fleetwood, making more headlines. The hotel would be constructed directly behind the Manor, which would eventually be razed. In the meantime, Stoltz would use it as an office.

In the months that followed, excavation was completed and a spur line to the nearest railroad tracks was put under construction to haul in the girder work. For some reason never

The old manor house that would become Augusta National's clubhouse.
Historic Golf Photos.

explained, work on the spur line was held up. But the Commodore endorsed his commitment to Augusta by enrolling his son, Fleetwood Courtwright Stoltz, in Richmond Academy, Augusta's outstanding prep school for boys.

Then, in, September, southern Florida was hit by the worst hurricane in its history. The Fleetwood Hotel was all but totally demolished, along with most of the others on Miami Beach. Commodore Stoltz filed for bankruptcy. As things turned out in court, it seems he had never actually owned the Berckmans tract on which he had planned his hotel. It had actually been owned by a holding company called the Washington Heights Development Company, which had agreed to turn over the land to Stoltz on the completion of his hotel.

The land stood undeveloped and unsold for five years. Then, on June 30, 1931, the *Chronicle* carried the news that the 365 acres of the Berckmans tract on the south side of Washington Road had been sold for $70,000 to the Fruitland Manor Corporation, the officers of which were not identified. Consequently, nobody in Augusta seemed to know, or care a whole lot during that second year of the Depression, who constituted the Fruitland Manor Corporation.

But it would not take them long to find out, and to care a whole lot.

On July 15, the *Chronicle* carried its largest headline since the Armistice of 1918: BOBBY JONES TO BUILD HIS IDEAL GOLF COURSE ON BERCKMANS' PLACE.

Two-thirds of page one were devoted to details of the project, with pictures of the site and another of Jones holding a set of plans with Dr. Alister Mackenzie, who would be the course architect. (Mackenzie's given name was misspelled "Alistair," a pardonable error considering that Mackenzie had actually been christened "Alexander.") Stories ran over to page two about the particulars of the sale, about the site itself and how well it would lend itself to a golf course, and included a long history of Jones's career. There was also a story, with O. B. Keeler's byline, that contained a statement by Jones about the club—which would be called Augusta National. Jones said:

I am joining with a group of friends as one of the organizers of a new club to be known as the Augusta National Golf Club. It is strictly a private undertaking and is in no sense a commercial project. Although my time now is largely devoted to the business of law, and I have retired forever from competitive golf, this great game will always be my hobby, and my ambition in connection with the Augusta enterprise is to help build a course which may possibly be recognized as one of the great golf courses of the world.

Augusta is in my home state. It has a singularly fine climate, and my experience in this city, in the Southeastern Open Championship last spring, convinced me that nowhere in this hemisphere was there anything to surpass the golfing conditions, in turf, greens or climate, offered by this immediate locality.

Of course I cannot deny that it is an idea very dear to my heart, to see in reality a golf course embodying the finest holes of all the great courses on which I have played. But I am not having this dream alone, or without the most expert collaboration. Dr. Mackenzie is the man who will actually design the course. His name needs no presentation to the American golfing public or the golfers of the world. I am happy to accompany him this morning on a tour of the property and to assume the role of consultant with him for this golf course. I know it is his ambition, and my earnest hope, to present a course that will find a place in North American golfing history as one of the layouts truly national in character and characteristics. English sportsmen and Canadians have been invited to join this club; and I am sure we shall have in Augusta a representative group of members from all over the world. This club, as I hope, is to be a truly national golf club.

Although the statement was accurate on the whole, the wording of it seems to have been hurriedly put together, almost as though it had been dictated by Jones to Keeler. For it contains Keeler's Victorian punctuation and several uses of the adjective "golfing," a word Jones didn't like and later came to view with distaste, seeing no reason why "golf" alone couldn't serve just as well. And, Jones never would have referred to the Southeastern Open as a "Championship."

What was important is that the statement was ambiguous about the design philosophy of the course. Jones never had any intention of seeing his dream of a course "embodying the finest holes of all the great courses on which I have played."

What Keeler might have said, and Jones certainly meant to say, was that Augusta National's course would embody "features" of the finest holes he had played. To actually copy the holes would have meant, as Jones would have to argue later, "literally to alter the face of the earth." At any rate, it was a statement he would spend months, even years, denying as journalists all over the world who knew little or nothing about golf-course architecture persisted in writing that Augusta National was a facsimile of the best eighteen holes Bobby Jones had ever played, particularly those in England and Scotland.

The lead article in the *Chronicle* went on to list local figures who were active in the project. They were Fielding

Wallace, president of the Augusta Country Club (and later a president of the USGA); Alfred S. Bourne, "capitalist"; and Thomas Barrett, Jr., a very active member of Augusta's Chamber of Commerce.

"Out-of-towners" involved were Grantland Rice, the New York sportswriter; Walton H. Marshall, president of the Vanderbilt Hotel in New York; William C. Watt, of Boston, chairman of the board of the United Drug Company; and Clifford Roberts, of New York City, an investment broker.

The key figure—as he would be within Augusta National for the next forty-seven years—was Clifford Roberts, a man about whom very little was known. Not much more is known about him today. He was a very private person.

Eight years older than Jones, Roberts had been born on March 6, 1894, on a farm near Morning Sun, a flyspeck on the map of Iowa sixty miles south of Cedar Rapids. His parents were Charles Roberts and the former Rebecca Scott Key, who was a distant cousin of Francis Scott Key, the American poet who wrote the words for "The Star-Spangled Banner." (By a curious coincidence, F. Scott Fitzgerald, whose first name was Francis, was also born to a distant cousin of the author.) Clifford was the second of what were to be five children altogether, an older and younger brother, who was followed, in 1900, by a twin sister and brother.

In 1905, when Clifford was eleven, the father moved the family to Palacios, Texas, a town not much larger than Morning Sun that sits on the coastline of the Gulf of Mexico midway between Galveston, to the northeast, and Corpus Christi, to the southwest. Here Charles Roberts sold real estate, and here Clifford, after barely graduating from high school after an argument with the school's principal, became a "drummer," or traveling salesman, for a now long-forgotten brand of wholesale men's suits. In 1913, his mother died, a suicide, and the family broke up, the father taking the younger children to Kansas City, Missouri, where he eventually remarried.

Clifford Roberts continued to sell suits on the road with a success that delighted his home office, so much so that he was permitted to take the summers off to visit his maternal grandfather, Dorias Key, with whom Clifford's older brother, Jack, was now living; both were being supported by the fruits of a vineyard near San Diego, California. A self-educated man, Dorias Key had a large library devoted mainly to biographies and autobiographies of the rich and famous. Now that he was a successful salesman, Clifford regretted that he had not been able to afford to go to college. So he began to devour his grandfather's library, concentrating on the biographies and autobiographies. The rich and the famous would hold a singular fascination for him for the rest of his life.

Clifford was twenty-three when the United States entered the First World War. Enlisting in the Army Medical Corps, he was sent to Camp Hancock, near Augusta, for basic training. He served for more than a year as an ambulance driver in France. In Paris, he met and began a vague relationship with a young woman named Suzanne Verdet, with whom, for a very good reason, he remained in contact for the rest of his days. Roberts credited Mlle. Verdet for saving his life, not during the war but ten years after it.

On a business trip to London in 1928, Roberts took the inaugural flight of a new airliner to Paris to resume his acquaintanceship with Suzanne. He was to return to London the next day on the same airliner. Suzanne insisted that he stay over in Paris an extra day, so delighted was she to see him. The airliner crashed that day in the English Channel. There were no survivors. Forty-odd years later, when Mlle. Verdet was confined to a nursing home in Garches, France, Roberts paid all her bills, an expense that continued to be taken care of in his will.

After the war, Roberts returned to Texas as a salesman. But with the reading he had now done about the rich and famous and the broadening of his mind while overseas, he knew his future lay in something grander than men's clothing. He began to dabble in oil leases. In 1921, when he was twenty-seven, the sale of some leases in eastern Texas netted him $50,000, an immense profit in those days. The financial pages in New York began referring to Roberts as the "Boy Wonder of Wall Street."

With his $50,000, Roberts bought a one-sixth partnership in Reynolds & Company, the brokerage firm now known as Dean Witter Reynolds, Inc., and opened an office at 120 Broadway. He was thirty-five when the Crash of '29 happened. He had been warned early in 1929 of the coming disaster by Melvin A. Traylor, a former president of the USGA who had been head of the First National Bank of Chicago and who would later become a very active member of Augusta National. Like a lot of others on Wall Street, though, Roberts could not believe Traylor, and so ended up losing a great deal of money, although he managed to hold on to his fractional partnership in Reynolds & Company.

Although not as hugely wealthy as many would come to think, Roberts had a knack for making wealthy men more wealthy than they already were. After the war, he had taken up golf, which he knew would help him make invaluable contacts as a "customer's man." By the midtwenties, Roberts was playing his golf at the Knollwood Country Club in New York's suburban Westchester County. There he met Walton Marshall, who, like Roberts, was keen on bridge and good at it. The two of them were often partners at the Two-Cent

Jones and Roberts at about the time Augusta National was being formed. Historic Golf Photos.

Bridge Club in Manhattan. In addition to operating the Vanderbilt Hotel in New York, Marshall also ran a chain of Vanderbilts, one of which was the Bon Air Vanderbilt in Augusta, where Jones stayed on several occasions to play some of his near-endless string of charity matches and on frequent visits to play recreational rounds in the winter when Atlanta became too cold. (Augusta sits in a valley, only 137 feet above sea level, or nearly 1,000 feet below Atlanta.)

Additionally, Jones had found that Augusta had not just one but two courses that were the equal of any in Atlanta. They were the Number One Course of the Augusta Country Club (it then had two courses) and the nearby course at the Forest Hills Ricker Hotel, which did not survive the Second

World War, the hotel becoming an army and then a veterans' hospital. (The Southeastern Open that Jones won in warming up for the Grand Slam had been played over both courses, thirty-six holes at each.)

Having met Walton Marshall in Augusta, Jones then began staying at the Vanderbilt whenever he was in New York. It was there that Marshall introduced Jones to Roberts, who, like everyone else who knew anything at all about golf, was a huge admirer, an admiration that was enhanced considerably by the fact that Jones, while far from rich, was internationally famous.

Soon afterward, Roberts became a frequent visitor to Augusta in the winter, playing golf at the Augusta Country Club, where he met Alfred Severn Bourne, who had a winter home there. Bourne's father had headed the Singer Sewing Machine Company, one of the giants that grew out of the Industrial Revolution. When his father died, Bourne's share of the enormous trust fund set up for the heirs was $25,000,000.

Like a lot of men of inherited ultrawealth, Bourne was self-conscious about his money and a bit shy in the company of others, mainly because he was constantly being pestered by salesmen or people looking for donations to charities, real and imagined. To insure his privacy, he regularly made cash gifts to the country club, gifts that kept it liquid, in return for which the club installed a separate locker room for his private use. Few members were invited in.

One of the few was Clifford Roberts.

In the meantime, a friendship between Roberts and Jones had developed, and Roberts became aware that Jones wanted some day to build a very private club. Jones explained that he had been finding it increasingly difficult to play even the most casual round of golf without a gallery in attendance, usually in the hundreds, often in the thousands. Additionally, he wanted to have a hand in helping design a course that would express a lot of his architectural ideas and that would be championship in every sense of the word, something that was sorely lacking anywhere in the South. Roberts filed Jones's ambitions in the tidy warehouse of his mind.

During one of his many golf junkets to Augusta, Roberts met Thomas Barrett, probably at the Bon Air Vanderbilt and possibly over a bridge game. Barrett had never played golf in his life, although he was active in other sports, having engaged the support of the Chamber of Commerce behind a number of athletic events in Augusta. Like so many millions of nongolfers in the country, he admired Jones immensely, an admiration that was increased all the more by having met him.

Just after Jones had made the public announcement of his retirement, he and Roberts had a short conversation in Atlanta about the idea of his private club. It was agreed that Augusta was a more logical place than Atlanta for it. To begin with, Jones was interested in a club where golf could be played primarily in the winter. Secondly, Augusta had a number of winter residents whose wealth had survived the stock market crash. The nucleus of a national membership could be built about them. In Atlanta, that seemed unlikely.

It was agreed that Roberts would handle the financing. Jones at that time was nearly broke, having spent most of his earnings playing in championships on both sides of the Atlantic. He had yet to select, let alone make money, from the avalanche of commercial propositions that was now overflowing his office. With the inestimable stature of Bobby Jones behind him, Roberts had few misgivings about the project. The Depression couldn't last forever.

Back in Augusta, Roberts felt that the most logical man to consult with first was Tom Barrett, active as he was in the Chamber of Commerce. Barrett immediately recalled the hullabaloo about Commodore Stoltz and the Augusta Fleetwood. He recommended that Roberts look into the property held by the Washington Heights Development company—Baron Berckmans's old Fruitlands Nurseries.

By now, it was the spring of 1931. Roberts telephoned Jones to come to Augusta as soon as possible so the two of them could look over the property. To be sure, Jones had seen the run-down nursery before. Having played so often at the Augusta Country Club, which adjoins it, he couldn't have helped but see it. But that view had been at the lowest point on the property, where Rae's Creek cuts across the southeast corner of the old nursery and disappears to the south. (Herbert Warren Wind would label it "Amen Corner" years later.) Now, for the first time, Jones was to drive through that honor guard of magnolias that leads to the Manor and then to look down on the flowering expanses from the lawn behind the house.

"I shall never forget my first visit to the property," Jones would write years later.

> The long lane of magnolias through which we approached was beautiful. The old manor house with its cupola and walls of masonry two feet thick was charming. The rare trees and shrubs of the old nursery were enchanting. But when I walked out on the grass terrace under the big trees behind the house and looked down over the property, the experience was unforgettable. It seemed that this land had been lying here for years waiting for someone to lay a golf course upon it. Indeed, it even looked as though it already were a golf course, and I am sure that one standing today

where I stood on this first visit, on the terrace overlooking the practice putting green, sees the property almost exactly as I saw it then. The grass of the fairways and greens is greener, of course, and some of the pines are a bit larger, but the broad expanse of the main body of the property lay at my feet then just as it does now.

For the rest of Jones's life, some of the most serene hours of that not very serene future were spent just gazing at that view.

An option on the property was obtained from Washington Heights Development at the price of $70,000, or just under $200 an acre, an eminently fair price on both sides, considering the times, the undeveloped nature of the land, and that the Manor was in such a state of disrepair as to be almost uninhabitable. Jones and Roberts could have bought the property for half that amount three years later.

To help underwrite the financing, Roberts first approached Alfred Bourne, asking for $5,000. At the mention of Bobby Jones as head of the venture, Bourne became strangely distressed. Then he explained. With Jones involved, Bourne wanted to underwrite the entire venture. But he had lost $10,000,000 almost overnight after the Crash. He was now temporarily short of cash, but pledged $25,000 to be paid within the year.

Bill Watt, the Boston drugstore executive who kept a winter home in Augusta, wrote a check instantly for $5,000. Others wrote out checks for $5,000 or $10,000 as soon as they were approached, beginning with Fielding Wallace. When Walton Marshall was asked for a $5,000 commitment, he insisted on matching Bourne's pledge of $25,000, not on behalf of his hotel chain but as an individual.

Such was the magic of the name Bobby Jones.

In a matter of weeks after Jones had let it be known that he wanted to start a golf club, Augusta National was financially off the ground, this little more than a year after Wall Street had undergone the worst panic in its history and when banks were beginning to close their doors with alarming accelera-tion. None of the underwriters had any doubts that Bobby Jones would keep the club airborne. His career, and especially the Grand Slam part of it, hadn't had time to come into focus as yet. But it was universally conceded that Bobby Jones could do anything he wanted connected to the game of golf. At a time when everybody seemed to be losing the cool they had in the twenties, Jones was keeping his *style gallant*.

Grantland Rice, who was one of the highest-paid writers in the world and more famous than most of the athletes he wrote about, had personally committed himself to Jones a year before, at whatever amount Jones wanted, site unseen, wher-ever it might be. His name would carry a lot of weight with potential members, and he was full of ideas for the new club.

The press would have a lot to do with making Augusta National the institution it would become, as Jones was humbly aware before the club ever got started. He knew that much of what he had done in golf might have been lost in overblown prose—or, at best, been historically distorted—had it not been for O. B. Keeler playing Boswell to his Dr. Johnson.

Keeler had covered all twenty-seven of the national cham-pionships in which Jones had played since boyhood. They had traveled more than 120,000 miles together by car, train, and boat, from coast to coast and three times to Europe. In hotel rooms Keeler had seen Jones doubled over with stomach pains, sometimes to the point of vomiting, or bursting into tears at no provocation, all from the nervous tension of playing the nearly impossible golf that the public expected of him. Jones wasn't sure where that golf was going to take him. He only knew that it was some place golf had never been. Keeler shared some of Jones's innermost thoughts and feelings at those times, but where Bobby's golf was going was one of the things both felt was best left unsaid.

After the Amateur Championship at Merion, Keeler wrote of Jones that the Grand Slam was a "granite fortress that he alone could take by escalade, and that others may attack in vain, forever." And when soon afterward Jones had announced that he was retiring, Keeler had written that so had he, figuratively. Although he would cover tournaments eloquently clear up till his death twenty years later, Keeler felt that golf thereafter had to be something of an anticlimax.

"Bobby Jones is not one in a million persons," Grantland Rice would write twenty-three years after the Grand Slam. "I should say he is one in ten million—or perhaps one in fifty million. The combination of Jones and Keeler is one in a hundred million."

With all the grand-scale optimism that was thrown behind the financing of Bobby Jones's Augusta National, one sour note was sounded. Jones had taken the stance that he should not ask anyone in Atlanta to help finance his club, now that the site for it had been chosen as Augusta. Roberts was to take only what was volunteered from that quarter. As it turns out, only one person from Atlanta was willing to become an underwriter. He was Harry Atkinson, founder of the Georgia Power Company, an elderly man who looked upon Jones with grandparental pride. When Jones had returned from the British Isles with both the Amateur and Open Championships that past June for his second parade up Broadway, Atkinson had chartered what amounted to a ferry boat for several hundred of Bobby's friends to greet the *Europa* as it sailed into New York harbor, just so they wouldn't go unnoticed among Manhattan's millions.

While Jones said nothing, everybody knew he was disappointed at the reception his club had received in his hometown. He offered to pledge himself for $5,000. But everybody else involved in the project from the start knew Jones had no money, what with his golf expenses over the past eight years and those at a time in life when he should have been getting a financial toehold somewhere. Besides, nobody could even hazard a guess at what his name and reputation had done to underwrite the club. Indeed, he *was* the club. So, he was looked upon as the last person who should contribute to it financially. But as the Depression got worse, not better, and his friends made financial sacrifices for the club, Jones put money into Augusta National over their objections. He insisted. If not actually putting more money into the club than Clifford Roberts, which he may well have, he put infinitely more into it than the two had first thought. While it had been agreed between them that Jones would attract friends from golf circles and Roberts from members of the financial community, not one member from that community was not also a personal friend of Jones's.

Other than old Harry Atkinson, Atlantans were miffed that Jones had not chosen his hometown for his dream course. But Jones was not after an intercity country club with tennis courts, a swimming pool, and some castle of a clubhouse complete with squash courts and a barn of a ballroom. He was after a national, indeed, *international*, golf club that would be a retreat for men of golf, a "house in the high woods," as Keeler had quoted Hilaire Belloc about Jones's retirement, where Jones could "grow to be old" and where "the men that were boys when I was a boy/Shall sit and drink with me."

Jones knew, and Roberts had wholeheartedly agreed, that he couldn't find that seclusion in a city growing as Atlanta was. The men he knew who would make the sort of members he was after would not come to any metropolis. But they would come to Augusta. It was not too big, not too fashionable, not too far out of the way.

And there had been precedents for why Jones thought his golf club would become recherché in Augusta and not in, say, Atlanta. The Old Course at St. Andrews had been sought after in a university town such as St. Andrews, but might not have been in nearby Edinburgh. Pine Valley had achieved a jewel-like quality in a New Jersey whistle stop once named Sumner, but might not have in nearby Philadelphia. And Cypress Point, the course he had been so struck by in California, had a stand-off elegance on the Monterey Peninsula it perhaps might not have had, Jones knew, were it farther up the coast in San Francisco.

No! If you had to pick a place in the South and in Georgia, Augusta was it, not Atlanta.

And so it was.

There never had been any question that the architect for Augusta National would be Alister Mackenzie. Johnny Goodman, the orphaned teenager who had gone to Pebble Beach on a drover's pass, had settled that problem for Jones unconsciously in the very first round of the 1929 Amateur Championship. With the underwriting for $70,000 to buy the Berckmanses' old nursery found without leaving Augusta, the money needed to build the golf course was obtained in a matter of weeks from Jones worshipers all over the country, particularly in the Northeast. Now that they had heard about it, golfers of every financial stripe wanted to join "Bobby's club," all of whom considered themselves personal friends and a number of whom couldn't afford to be underwriters. So, for the future, membership was put on an "invitation only" basis. That way nobody who was not a personal friend of Jones's would have his feelings hurt by being turned down by a membership committee. Initiation fees had been set at a nominal $350, annual dues at $60. For some of the younger members Jones wanted to join, ways were found around the underwriting minimum of $5,000.

Mackenzie was able to start work on the course almost immediately. While he was a world-famous architect, he was not in the business just for the money. He had designed very few courses in the United States, although others were as far-flung as Melbourne, Buenos Aires, and Montevideo. Just across the bay from Cypress Point, where he lived in Santa Cruz, he had designed Pasatiempo, one of the great unheralded courses in America. And he designed two courses for Ohio State University, in Columbus, which he never lived to see constructed.

One reason Mackenzie had not been kept overly busy was that he refused to design a course that would cost more than $100,000 to construct. Miraculously, he would come close to meeting that figure at Augusta National. For in following Jones's wishes that the course be kept playable for the underwriters and future members, expenses that Mackenzie had never encountered before were added. Fairways, for one item, ended up covering eighty acres, as opposed to the thirty or forty most courses had, and still have. Also, the greens would cover more than 100,000 square feet, an unheard-of total at that time. Around each green would be a thirty-six-inch collar of turf, to be as carefully tended as the putting surfaces themselves. Soil was conditioned with a care reserved only for Japanese gardens, a special humus from Florida, donated by the president of the New York Stock Exchange, having been expensively shipped to Augusta by the trainload. Many of the results of the money spent would never be seen. They would be underground. Mackenzie was told to use the last word in drainage installations, and the whole course was piped with a watering system, one of the first in the world.

This, after all, was "Bobby's course."

Although Mackenzie had been told to spare no expense on this golf course that was expected to live for the ages, it was built in remarkably short time—about a year—all for a number of economic reasons that seem as remote today as those under which the Pyramids were built. Although the construction engineer, a man from New York named Wendell P. Miller, had been told to pay day workers a dollar a day, which was the going rate at the time, Miller found that they were readily available at fifty cents because of the Depression. In fact, many hard-put farm laborers volunteered to work for twenty-five cents. And all of them labored, according to the workweek of the times, from "can to can't," meaning from the time in the morning they could see what they were doing until the time in the evening when they no longer could. The "eight-hour day" had not been thought of anywhere in the country, nor consequently the "forty-hour week." Most men worked at whatever they did six days out of the week. Even Wall Street was now open only five days a week for the first time in its hustling, hectic past. But that was enforced, not requested. Trading on the stock market had come to an almost disastrous standstill.

The times were tough. And they were going to get tougher.

Jones and Mackenzie had surely looked over the old Berckmans property together long before July 15 of 1931, when the *Augusta Chronicle* had first made headlines of the news that Jones was going to "Build His Ideal Golf Course" on it. Even so, they laid out the course in what may have been record time.

Much of the time saved was due to the rapport between Jones and Mackenzie, which may still stand as unique between a front-rank player and a first-rate architect. While Jones inarguably knew more about the playing values of a golf course than anybody then alive, if not since, he knew where his talents ended and Mackenzie's began. "No man learns to design a golf course," Jones would write years later, "simply by playing golf, no matter how well."

Jones had a deep respect for Mackenzie's architectural eye, which would see golf beauty in virgin land that few persons since him have been able to detect so quickly. The thirteenth

Jones overseeing early construction work on the course. Historic Golf Photos.

hole—that heroic "par–four-and-a-half" that was to become the most photogenic and perhaps the most famous hole on the course—was designed by Mackenzie at practically the instant he first saw the valley it sits in and the tiny creek that babbles along the left-hand side of it. (The creek is often mistakenly referred to as Rae's Creek, which actually winds off the property behind the twelfth green.)

Bowing to Mackenzie's eye for innate beauty, Jones stood aside while Mackenzie routed the holes—something Jones had never had call to do before, anyway. He would get around to putting the shot values into each hole after Mackenzie showed him where each should be and how all of them should interconnect.

Mackenzie had a number of problems removed for him in routing the course. One was that he did not have to listen to the blandishments of real-estate developers, who can suddenly turn into experts on golf-course architecture overnight, some of them without ever having played the game. While Jones and Roberts admittedly toyed with the idea of selling home-sites on the property, Jones would never have permitted a home, however grand, to encroach on his monumental Augusta National. One cottage was built by a local member near what is now the second tee. But, as a matter of future policy, Jones and Roberts abandoned all further notions that Augusta National would become a development. In time, that first house was bought by the club and razed.

Soon afterward, two members suggested they would like to solicit funds through a national campaign to build a monument to Jones on the grounds. They thought a huge statue of him ought to be erected near the entrance. Jones was horrified. He told the membership firmly that the golf course would be monument enough to whatever anybody wanted to pay tribute. In succeeding years, all gifts to the club in the form of books or other memorabilia were referred to the USGA for its library and museum. Still, golfists and sightseers started dropping by just to look at the course, eventually at the rate of two hundred a day. A gate, to be guarded round the clock, had to be installed. They still come by at a steady rate to see "the course that Bobby built."

Free to lay out the course in any way he saw fit, Mackenzie could let his fancy fly. He had very few inhibitions about how long or how short a hole ought to be. For one reason, he had no preconceptions about par, which he considered a figment of the USGA's imagination. To Mackenzie's way of thinking, "par" as such was just an a priori argument as to how the game ought to be played. Mackenzie went along with the old Scottish theory that an ideal round of golf ought to add up to "level fours." How those fours added up was immaterial. Not knowing how they would add up was what gave golf its "spirit of adventure." Handicap committees took something away from that spirit by telling you how you were *supposed* to add them up.

Once, an amateur acquaintance told Mackenzie that he should make a point of playing a certain golf course.

"Why?" asked Mackenzie, taken back by the man's seeming enthusiasm.

"Would you believe it?" said the man. "Nobody's ever been able to break par on the course."

"My goodness," Mackenzie replied. "What on earth's wrong with it?"

Both Jones and Mackenzie were "extravagant admirers," as Jones put it, of the Old Course at St. Andrews. Consequently, they both wanted to simulate seaside conditions as much as the terrain would allow. Thus, Augusta National's fairways would bump and roll every which way, as though eons ago they had been buried beneath the sea. Mounds were used in place of the bunkers resorted to by ordinary courses. In this respect, Augusta National would stand toweringly unique among the world's championship courses. The original layout would have only twenty-nine bunkers at a time when anything less than a hundred was considered no golf course at all.

Only a man of Bobby Jones's disciplined tastes could have conceived such a golf course, and only a man of Alister Mackenzie's disciplined imagination could have brought it off. Mackenzie's architectural creed was to build courses for the "most enjoyment for the greatest number." And Jones's uppermost thought about golf courses was that their primary purpose was "to give pleasure, and that to the greatest possible number of players, without respect to their capabilities." The most intelligent way to fuse both philosophies was by limiting bunkers, particularly off the tees, now that rough had all but been eliminated and greens made so huge that they seemed impossible to miss.

The end result was utter minimalism, and it would revolutionize golf architecture in America. The problem would no longer be what to put into a golf course but what to leave out, although some architectural theorists still haven't got the message. Some never will.

Mackenzie's original sketch for the course was not discovered until 1983, when it was found framed but ignored in a clubhouse apartment of a member who, as it happens, died the following year. It was probably ignored because it was never used or, at any rate, not in its entirety. True to his principles, Mackenzie did not list par on any hole. But the yardages on each hole, using the USGA's criteria for par, called for the course to have had a total par of 73. As a professional

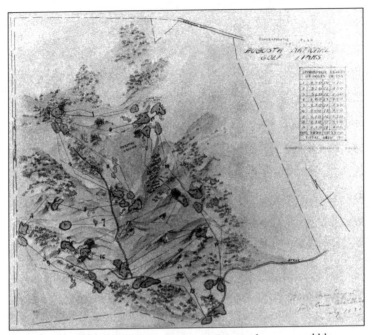

Mackenzie's original sketch for the course. Many changes would be made to it. Alston & Bird.

Scotsman, Mackenzie would have ignored that figure and said the course played to "level fours."

To begin with, the fifth hole was somewhat longer than it now is, calling for a par of five.

The sixth was also longer by about twenty-five yards, but would have still been a par-three.

Par at the seventh would have remained at four, but the hole was much shorter and easier, its green lying in that part of the fairway where a pro could easily drive with today's ball.

Another hole that was much shorter was the tenth, the green for which lay below the fairway bunker that is there now.

At the top of the hill, near where the tenth green is today, was the eleventh tee.

The thirteenth hole was slightly shorter, and would have been just over the borderline as a par-five, as it still is, now that it has been lengthened and the USGA's standards have grown longer.

The fourteenth had a fairway bunker that has since been removed.

The fifteenth was much shorter and would have played to a par of four.

The sixteenth was much shorter, but the seventeenth was much longer, playing off the tee into what is now fifteen's fairway. You then approached the green from the right of the bunker that now sits in front of it, giving the hole a par of five.

Eighteen would have played much as it does today, except that the fairway bunkers would not be put in until much later.

But at eighteen, you weren't finished! Mackenzie had designed a nineteenth hole—literally. From the eighteenth green, you walked to the left and slightly down the hill toward what would become a practice range. You then played a short par-three up the hill to the right of the manor house. The green would have been where the gigantic practice putting green now is.

Ridiculous as such a hole seems today, there had been a precedent for Mackenzie's nineteenth. It was known previous to Augusta National as a "bye hole," and might not only have been tacked on to the eighteenth but shoehorned in somewhere along the back nine, say, between the sixteenth green and the seventeenth tee, where the original course at Congressional Country Club, outside Washington, D.C., and where Tommy Armour had been the pro, then had one. The point of the hole was to allow for an extra wager, in Augusta National's case perhaps to play for double or nothing.

Whatever the purpose, the hole was never built, probably because Jones thought it interfered with the symmetry of the course. It was too disproportionate, too out of harmony with the classicism he was after.

Mackenzie's contribution to Augusta National was now largely finished. Jones would take over from here—in the fall, winter, and spring of 1931–32. He would hit hundreds upon hundreds of experimental shots to see if each fairway had the sweep he was after, if every bunker struck just the right amount of fear in the heart, if every green accepted a well-hit shot and rejected a poor one. Using his own words, he wanted to see if the course could give pleasure "to the

Jones hits one of the hundreds of experimental shots he made while helping design Augusta National. Historic Golf Photos.

greatest possible number of players, without respect to their capabilities."

In that regard, Jones was uniquely qualified, certainly more than any golfer before him and possibly any since. He could not only carve a championship layout into pieces with his own knifelike shots, he had enormous empathy with those golfers who couldn't break 80 anywhere, and even with those who couldn't break 90 or 100. While those pros and amateurs he had competed against in championships seldom played with anybody other than each other between events, Jones went home to East Lake and often played with hopeless hackers. At his law office, he was constantly being interrupted by his father, who would burst in to exhibit some technicality of the swing that he felt sure, in downtown Atlanta, would make him almost as good a player as his son was at East Lake. Young Bob would listen patiently, and then smile knowingly, as though he were the father. He knew from experience that there wasn't any "secret" to a game as mysterious as golf.

Jones would often tell on himself a story that illustrates how uncondescending he was toward the durable duffer. It seems that one of his high-handicap friends had made an eagle-two on a par-four hole. After telling Jones about it, Jones asked him what club he had used for his second shot. "A four-wood," the man said.

"A *four*-wood?" Jones said in astonishment. "Why, I've never used more than a nine-iron on that hole."

"You ever make a two?" the man said.

Chapter 7:
The Augusta
National Invitation

Alister Mackenzie would never see Augusta National in its finished form. He last visited the site in the summer of 1932, when the course was completed but still had no grass. After a trip to Scotland in 1933, he returned to Santa Cruz and fell seriously ill. He died in January of 1934.

It seems safe to say that Mackenzie approved of the alterations Jones had made after those hundreds of experimental shots, shots that, considering who was making them, gave Augusta National playing values no other as yet untested course in the world could have. The major change Jones made had been turning seventeen from a par-five into a par-four. No doubt Mackenzie didn't care one way or another that Jones had eliminated his nineteenth hole. It had been just so much icing on a cake that didn't need any.

One alteration will forever remain a mystery. Jones reversed the nines, with what is now the tenth hole becoming the first. In fact, that this had been a reversal and not Mackenzie's original routing was not known until Mackenzie's 1932 sketch was unearthed in 1983. Jones had never mentioned the switch to anybody alive in 1983, and whether he did so with Mackenzie's approval cannot be known. But a qualified guess would be that Jones thought that Mackenzie's back nine, when actually built with Jones's other alterations, was measurably easier than his front, what with the old tenth, eleventh, fifteenth, and sixteenth holes, which have since been turned from relatively platitudinous holes into some of the more challenging. Mackenzie's old front nine would then make for a more stirring finish. Whatever the reasons, the course would open for play with the tenth hole as the first.

Purely for historical purposes, it was decided not to tear down the manor house, with its walls of "artificial rock" fully eighteen inches thick, although they had been cracked by the "Charleston earthquake" of 1886. The house had fourteen rooms, seven on each floor, and a cupola. One of the rooms on the first floor was turned into a kitchen, the original kitchen having been in a separate building outside, probably to keep the house itself cooler in Augusta's sizzling summers. The building had to be fully restored in 1938 at a cost way beyond that of a new clubhouse, which might not have been done at all if it hadn't been for a gift of $20,000 from a New York member named Bartlett Arkell, president of the Beech-Nut Packing Company, an incongruous extrovert who stood five feet five, weighed 250 pounds, ate and drank like Diamond Jim Brady, and owned one of the finest collections of paintings by Dutch masters in America.

One of the rooms on the first floor became an office for the club's first manager, who turned out to be one of Prosper Berckmans's sons, called Allie. Both Allie and his older brother, Louis, had been brought back to the property by Jones and Roberts, just for old-times' sake, and both then decided they would like to live out their days there, although neither played golf. Louis, in fact, joined the club, and served as its horticultural adviser. With Louis's invaluable horticultural background to guide them, Jones and Roberts decided to name each hole on the course after a flowering plant or tree. Louis made sure every hole was adorned in an off-stage way with the variety it was named after. And they are so named today: Tea Olive, Flowering Peach, Yellow Jasmine, and so on.

Jones gave a lot of thought to who should be the club's first professional. Uppermost in his mind was that the pro would have to be a gentleman in every sense. Secondly, he would have to be someone who enjoyed teaching. Thirdly, it would help matters if he were or had been a player of some note, although Jones did not believe that one talent necessarily qualified you for the other. He gave Roberts a list of three names: The first was veteran Macdonald Smith, a native of Carnoustie, Scotland, then living in Los Angeles, who had a swing so graceful that Tommy Armour had once said that he treated the turf "as though it were an altar cloth." The second name was Willie Macfarlane, who had beaten Jones in the play-off for the 1925 United States Open at Worcester Country Club, in Massachusetts. The third was Ed Dudley, who had just turned thirty, had been born in Georgia, and had won a dozen major tournaments, although never a national championship. Dudley was then professional at the Philadelphia Country Club, a lucrative job in its own right. He was the first approached, and he leaped at the opportunity, especially since he could serve both clubs, as Augusta National was closed during the summers.

Dudley would be Augusta National's pro for twenty-seven years. As popular with other pros as he was with the members, he would serve as president of the PGA of America seven years in a row.

At the beginning of 1933, the club had only eighty members, almost all of them from out of town and most of them from the Northeast. Some of them didn't know each other, and several of them had friends who wanted to join but who didn't know either Roberts or Jones personally. Although a few members had already started playing the course that past December, the club had had no formal opening. In New York—where headquarters for the club might just as well have been at that time—Roberts and Grantland Rice put their heads together.

They decided to hold a party. It would be "Dutch treat." Each member and his guest would contribute $100 toward expenses. Roberts arranged train transportation from Pennsylvania Station. Business was so off that the Pennsylvania Railroad not only supplied Pullman cars but threw in two club cars and two diners for good measure. Included in the $100 ticket was not only transportation all the way to Augusta and back but also three days' stay at the Bon Air Vanderbilt with meals (thanks to Walton Marshall) and transportation to and from the club, plus all the bootleg whiskey you could drink. The Depression was getting deeper, and things were dirt cheap.

There were a hundred men exactly in the Augusta party, two-thirds of them club members. The rest were their personal friends, potential members all. At Augusta National, Jones charmed the argyles off those who had never met him and left them bug-eyed with his golf shots. What that didn't accomplish, the bootleg whiskey did. Scotch at that period tasted like iodine—indeed, might have been made from it—and bourbon was hard to distinguish from gin, both of them having usually been distilled in bathtubs. The only real liquor a Southern gentleman would then drink was corn whiskey, slightly aged in the backwoods of Georgia. It had a kick few

Yankees had ever experienced, and Jones would recall with a smile years later how much it had to do with getting the club off the ground.

The weather was miserable—cold and rainy. To take the party's minds off it, tents at both the first and tenth tees were set up, each with a keg of corn whiskey. It wasn't long before nobody cared if it snowed.

Jones had wanted to discuss some business matters, now that he had most of the membership together for the first time, and so he had arranged a dinner at the Bon Air. When dessert was finished and the cigars had been passed, Jones got to his feet, papers in hand, as though he were about to address a courtroom. He never got to say a word.

The usually quiet Grantland Rice suddenly rose from his chair, interrupted Jones's opening remarks, and demanded to be heard. Jones, who considered Rice a candidate for sainthood, could do nothing but yield. Rice then went on to explain to the group that he had joined a number of promising clubs in the past, some of which went broke because they had become too entangled in meetings, resulting in a clash of egos such meetings among business leaders engender. He did not want that to be the fate of Augusta National.

Nobody would argue with Grantland Rice about a golf club; he belonged to too many of them. Without waiting for a reply, Rice then proposed that Augusta National be run by Jones and Roberts in any way they saw fit. All in favor were asked to stand and vote. Everybody in the room rose as one to their feet. There was a chorus of "ayes."

At that moment, it may be said in retrospect, Augusta National truly came into its own. For it has been the history of practically all successful golf clubs, both in this country and abroad, that they were run in an autocratic manner, usually benevolently, but sometimes not. Pine Valley would be ruled for more than thirty years by John Arthur Brown, a Philadelphia lawyer who had the body of an oarsman, a foghorn voice just as imposing as himself, and was an autocrat only if your idea of an autocrat was Henry VIII at his head-chopping best. Seminole, near Palm Beach, Florida, would have its members dictated to by a man named Chris Dunphy, who was the administrator for one of the largest estates among its famed society and, consequently, one of its social lions. Dunphy went so far as to make matches between Seminole's members and then dictate the handicaps they should play to, one of the highest being his own. There were numerous other golf autocracies that would survive the Depression simply because that's what they were.

In Jones and Roberts, Augusta National would have the perfect combination for leadership. Jones would be the only president the club would ever have; "in perpetuity" after his death. But he was constitutionally incapable of being autocratic, even with his children. So Roberts, who had the granite personality and now the cavalier attitude toward the rich and famous such a role entails, would act as his majordomo. As yet, that job wouldn't amount to much. But within a year it would be a job that would either bind Augusta National together or tear it asunder.

Roberts bound it together.

Satisfied that he had a championship course on his hands by the spring of 1933, Jones listened with interest to a suggestion by one of the members that Augusta National play host to a future United States Open, which had never been played south of Washington, D.C. One of the reasons Jones had started Augusta National was to bring a front-rank course to the South. It seemed altogether fitting that such a course should now become the site for the South's first national championship.

But there were obstacles that could not be overcome, and they immediately become obvious. The USGA had traditionally played the Open in late June or early July, sometimes stretching it clear into mid-July. The heat in Augusta at that time of year could be unbearable. Temperatures in July when the thirteenth hole was being built—the low point on the course—had been recorded in excess of 110 degrees. Thus, the championship would have to be held not later than April, a date everybody knew would be unacceptable to the USGA before it was even suggested.

Furthermore, the town then had a population of only sixty thousand, a large proportion of which were either black or mill workers (or both), neither of whom could be expected to support something as sophisticated as a golf championship, even a national one.

Last but by no means least, Bobby Jones would not play in an Open Championship, at his club or anybody else's, ever. That was final and irrevocable. And without Jones—if ticket sales were any indication—a USGA championship was beginning to be viewed as no attraction at all, Amateur or Open. Gate receipts for the 1931 Open, without Jones in the field, had been a paltry $12,700, and were still falling. The idea of the Open Championship at Augusta National was therefore dropped almost as abruptly as it had been brought up.

Still, not having a major event at Augusta National seemed like an enormous waste, what with the name "Bobby Jones" behind it and a membership almost entirely from the populous Northeast, many of whom had distinguished backgrounds within the USGA. And Jones was determined that Augusta National should do something constructive for the South. He may have been a man of the world, but his roots were deep in Dixie.

Cliff Roberts had never been a man to let a good idea slip through his fingers. Almost immediately after the notion of an Open Championship had been abandoned, he suggested that Augusta National invent a tournament of its own. He argued,

Cover from the program for what would become The Masters Tournament.
Historic Golf Photos.

altogether logically, that such a membership would find it not much more of a problem to operate an annual event of the club's own than one of somebody else's occasionally. What's more, such an event would put the club in a stronger position to decline proposals for outside tournaments or championships, which both he and Jones well knew would soon be laid at Augusta National's doorstep.

He suggested that the event be labeled the "Masters Tournament."

Jones liked the idea straight off. But he objected to the title. "Masters Tournament" he thought was too presumptuous for an event of the club's own making. He particularly didn't like the name for another reason he found egotistical. It had been suggested that he play in it, since it could not be construed as a championship in any sense. With hardly a hundred members, the Augusta National Golf Club could not call itself a recognized golf organization, even if it wanted to, however far it might try to stretch the public's imagination with Bobby Jones as its president.

Jones insisted that the event be called the Augusta National Invitation Tournament. And so it was—thereby making Jones paint himself into a corner no amount of logic could get him out of. Since Jones was to be the host and, as such, the man who would issue the invitations to those he wanted to play, he himself could not be so impolitic as not to play with them. Such a posture was too stiff for Jones as a gentleman, too graceless as a Southern one. He had at first ignored the argument that his actual playing was needed to make the tournament a financial success. But he couldn't ignore his duty as a host. He was constitutionally incapable of being aloof. Besides, he secretly relished playing again with his old pals, now that there weren't any titles on the line.

That he would accept no prize money was the sine qua non of the whole argument.

All these decisions about the Augusta National Invitation had been made in New York City. Nobody could see why the first event should not be staged in Augusta the following year, 1934. Grantland Rice suggested that the dates chosen should be in the last week of March. At that time, all the major-league baseball teams would be working their way north from spring training camps in Florida. With them would be most of the top sportswriters, all of whom would be anxious to write about Bobby Jones playing golf once again. That first tournament was going to need all the publicity it could get.

Even with Jones back in the headlines, it would take some doing to sell enough tickets in a town the size of Augusta. Spectators would have to be lured from Atlanta, Savannah, Macon, Columbia, Charleston, and Charlotte, none of which was exactly around the corner. Once again, it was impossible to overestimate the power of Bobby Jones's appeal. As things turned out, people drove all the way from Birmingham, nearly four hundred miles away on those old roads, and from Nashville, nearly five hundred—just for the day.

Cliff Roberts agreed to act as tournament chairman. Jones would have it no other way, and Roberts would serve as such until his death. Nobody argues that without him the Augusta National Invitation would never have become The Masters Tournament or that The Masters Tournament would never have become what it is. A demon at detail, he had a memory like a flip-file and fingers that could find what he wanted with just a snap. Most importantly, perhaps, he didn't give a damn what you thought of him while he was doing what he thought had to be done.

First off, Roberts recruited an assistant in a wealthy member named Jay Monroe, who was also a very active member at the Baltusrol Golf Club, in New Jersey, which had played host to a number of national golf events. At that time, Monroe was also one of the few members in those precarious times who could spare six weeks a year to help run a golf tournament.

Roberts then made a number of innovations unheard of in tournament golf. Rather than use local police and deputies for crowd control, for example, he hired uniformed men from the Pinkerton Agency, which had never been called on for a sports event before. (Today, sports assignments account for 75 percent of Pinkerton's business.) Augusta National then had no fence around it, and Roberts knew the local lawmen had too many friends they would let in free.

From the outset, Roberts determined that nobody, not even press or photographers, would be allowed within the ropes that were strung in a semicircle behind every tee and every green, this so the paying spectators, who would always come first at Augusta, would have an uninterrupted view of play. That was a decision not calculated to endear him with the invaluable newspapermen, especially since Granny Rice was a member and O. B. Keeler a confidant of Jones's. But it was farsighted. As The Masters Tournament, the Augusta National Invitation would eventually have nearly twice the press representation of any other tournament or championship in the world. There were a lot of things Cliff Roberts would do that were not calculated to endear him to others as the tournament would wear on, some of them of questionable intelligence. But nobody would ever deny that he had vision.

Jay Monroe suggested, and Roberts heartily concurred, that there should be no volunteer help during the tournament, outside the few local members and those from out of town who could spare a week off. However slight the help, everybody who had a hand in operating the tournament—marshals, soldiers, students—would be paid accordingly. Thus, from the very beginning, Roberts would have iron control over who would and who wouldn't work for him. And he would use it.

Jones and Roberts were both adamant that the tournament would be used to promote nothing outside the game of golf, and nothing commercial inside it. Every penny realized from the event would be used to improve future tournaments: prize money, gallery facilities, the golf course itself. It was a tough-minded decision, for it ruled out organized charities. (Later, some smaller, less recognized ones were contributed to very quietly.)

Parking for spectators would be free; daily pairing sheets would be given away.

The tournament—four rounds at stroke play, naturally—would be played over a leisurely four days, Thursday through Sunday, not just the three then in use in other parts of the country (mainly to skirt the blue laws still in effect in some cities that prohibited athletic events on Sunday but also because of some Calvinistic hangover that frowned upon golf being played on the Sabbath).

There would be no entry fee. This, after all, was a get-together of Bobby Jones's friends. And he had a lot of them, way more, in fact, than even Augusta National was aware of. Under whatever name it might be played, the Augusta National Invitation was on its historic way.

CHAPTER 8:
THE MASTERS
TOURNAMENT

From its very start, the first of what would be The Masters Tournaments was accepted hungrily by the public, who took to it in the spirit of a festival. Franklin Delano Roosevelt had been elected President in 1932 by a landslide vote (and inaugurated exactly twelve months ago that March) based on his promise to get the economy back on its feet. While the stock market was still reeling, there was nevertheless celebration in the national air. For one thing, Prohibition had been repealed in December of 1933, and with it disappeared a lot of lawlessness and the national guilt over drinking illegal alcohol, contrary to the devil-may-care way the Roaring Twenties have since been depicted.

A check of license plates throughout the tournament by Pinkerton men in the vast parking lot at the northwest corner of Augusta National's property showed that spectators had come from thirty-eight states and Canada. Evidently, a lot of them had come for more than the day. Where most of them slept while in Augusta was anybody's guess, some of them probably in their cars. The Bon Air Vanderbilt was the only hotel of any size, and it had been taken over mainly by contestants, whom Walton Marshall had given a special rate of five dollars a night. Another, smaller, more commercial hotel downtown was The Richmond, and there were a few quaint inns, like The Partridge, which had been built on the side of a hill across the street from the Bon Air years before it and whose floors even then were beginning to sag. Housing would be a problem at the tournament for another thirty years.

A bed to sleep on or not, people came in waves of early traffic that choked Augusta's streets. All of them came for the same reason. They wanted to see Bobby Jones play golf again. Never mind that the Augusta National Invitation was not a national championship. They would have come to see The Emperor play once more if the trophy had been a Hoover button.

The press turnout was the largest since any of the championships of the Grand Slam, four years before. According to Western Union, newsmen would file eighteen thousand more words than had been filed the previous year at the United States Open, which had been won by Johnny Goodman, the amateur who had put out Jones at Pebble Beach in 1929 and had thereby, in a roundabout way, precipitated Augusta National and this very tournament.

Tom Barrett, the Chamber of Commerce dynamo who had brought the old Berckmans nursery to Jones and Roberts's attention, was on his way to being elected Augusta's mayor, undoubtedly due to his role in bringing Augusta National, and now this nationally recognized golf tournament, to the community. Barrett had got wind that the event was at first to be called the "Masters Tournament," and he was disappointed that the title had not been approved by Jones. He thought it catchy, something that would fit hand in the public glove with the city of Augusta. He confided his disappointment to a local newspaper friend, who wrote up a story that was passed around press headquarters, then on the upstairs veranda of the clubhouse. Other newsmen liked the name, too, and so began referring to it as the "tournament of Masters" and as the "Masters tournament," without a capital *T*.

So, contrary to Jones's wishes, the first Augusta National Invitation Tournament was actually written up as "Masters

Tommy Armour, Walter Hagen, and Gene Sarazen stand by while Jones drives off first tee in a practice round for an early Masters Tournament. Historic Golf Photos.

Tournament" in some form or another throughout the country. It was going to be a hard name for Jones to get rid of. But, then, he never liked the name "Bobby," either.

The tournament had a field with the quality if not the depth of any championship in the country, thanks once more to the magnetism of Jones. Walter Hagen was there, along with other star professionals who had successfully made the transition from hickory to steel shafts, such as Bobby Cruickshank, the "Wee Scot"; Macdonald Smith, of the classic form; Willie Macfarlane, who had surprised himself by beating Jones for that 1925 Open Championship; Al Watrous, an old championship buddy from Detroit; Leo Diegel, the dazzling shot-maker; and dashing Johnny Farrell, who had defeated Jones in a play-off for the 1928 Open Championship. There were others who had played with hickory but who would find their real games with steel: Horton Smith, Craig Wood, Harold "Jug" McSpaden, Jimmy Hines, Denny Shute, Johnny Revolta, Sam Parks, Ky Laffoon, Henry Picard, Harry Cooper, Billy Burke, Olin Dutra, plus many whose names were yet to become familiar.

The British contingent was not what had been hoped, but only what was to be expected, now that the Depression had spread worldwide. Neither were the amateur entries as strong as Jones would have liked, not unexpectedly, for much the same reason. Then, too, the dates chosen—March 22 through March 25—were well in advance of the amateurs' tournament season. Those in the North, where nine-tenths of the championship amateurs lived, hadn't taken their clubs off the racks since the previous fall.

The most notable absentee was Gene Sarazen, who had added to his British Open in 1932 by also winning his second United States Open, and had won his third PGA Championship the year before this inaugural Augusta event. Sarazen was fulfilling a previous commitment, an exhibition tour through South America. But he had promised his friend Bob Jones that he would play the following year.

By way of another innovation at the tournament, it had been decided to play the field in pairs rather than the standard groups of three. It was thought, and wisely so, that spectators could see more shots and have a better idea with twosomes of what was happening in the tournament generally. Besides, such pairings would speed up play. Jones, for one, despised slow play, seeing no reason why a round of golf should ever take more than three hours. While he never said so, there was no question that many of his competitive rounds had been a stroke or two higher because controlling his enormous galleries was such a problem, making him wait frustratingly between shots while marshals pushed the crowds back and then often forced him to shoot down an alleyway of spectators. He had always had a fear of injuring somebody, and he considered the fact that he never did one of the luckiest aspects of his career.

Jones was paired in the opening round with Paul Runyan, a slightly built pro from Arkansas with a hitch in his backswing and form otherwise as unorthodox as Jones's was textbook. But Runyan had a short game that more than made up for his lack of length, and he could handle a three-wood more accurately than some pros could an eight-iron. Awkward though he might have looked, Runyan had been leading money-winner for the past two years and would go on to win two PGA Championships. To show how deep the Depression had gone, his winnings that second year had been a measly $6,767 as opposed to Sarazen's $21,500 in 1930. An accountant told Runyan afterward that the total had been only ten dollars more than his expenses.

With Runyan, Jones drew what seemed like every spectator on the course as he strode to the first tee. He had enjoyed himself immensely in the practice rounds, playing once again with his old pro pals. But he knew now that the fun was over. Just before he teed off, he had found his hands trembling as he wrapped the middle finger of his right hand with tape where he had a tendency to develop a callus. He also felt that old "vacant sensation" in his stomach. But neither sign of nervousness bothered him mentally. Indeed, he welcomed them. They usually meant he had a good round on deck.

Jones cracked a drive 270 yards down the middle of the first fairway, tens of yards in front of Runyan. A pitch, a putt, and then a tap-in made his par. On the second hole, or what is now the eleventh, his approach putt was a twenty-five-footer, which he tried to sweep to the hole, in his customary fashion, so that it would die in or at it. But he jabbed the ball six feet past. He jerked the next putt, too. Still, it went in.

Right then, Jones felt that something was radically wrong.

On the par-five fourth hole—now the thirteenth—he faded a two-wood off a sidehill lie nicely onto the green, bringing a roar from the gallery. He got down in two putts for his first birdie to go one under par.

Yet he still felt strangely out of championship character, as though he were miraculously walking on water.

On the next tee, the whir of a movie camera made him stop in the middle of his backswing. Ordinarily, Jones could interrupt his *downswing*, so much in control did he keep the clubhead. But for the first time in memory, something outside that spotlight he was so used to had unsettled him. (Years ago, when a little girl had poked her head through the gallery as Jones was almost at impact, he had been able to top his shot on purpose.)

Jones readdressed the ball uneasily, and pushed his drive into the rough. He knew at that instant that something had gone out of his game, forever. Nothing so inconsequential had ever unnerved him before. He had started off innumerable rounds dangerously and then somehow pulled them out of the fire. But he knew now that this round wasn't going to be one of them and that there would never be any more.

The Emperor didn't have any clothes on. Only, this Emperor *knew* it.

Jones scored a 76, added a 74 the next day, and then finished the last two rounds with a brace of par 72s, finishing in a tie for thirteenth. Despite those mediocre scores, Jones made more headlines and took up more column space in the newspapers than those who were leading. The public thought he had been merely "off his stick," having stood outside the championship wars for four years.

But Jones knew better. It was all over. Although he would play in eleven more of what would soon rightly be labeled The Masters Tournaments, he would not be one of those masters, never to finish higher than that ignominious thirteenth; in fact, not as high.

When in November of 1930 he had quit "the memorable scene on which he nothing common did," as *The New York Times* spoke of his major national championships, actually Jones had quit all competitive golf, spiritually. For major national championships were the only competitive golf his instincts could rise for, his nerves could settle down to, his intellect could cut its way through. Mere tournaments were something for which he could seldom bring his best golf forward, having once dissipated five strokes of an eighteen-stroke lead right there in Augusta for that Southeastern Open in the year of the Grand Slam, no less.

It wasn't that Jones had lost his nerves. After all, he was only thirty-two. To the contrary, he had found his nerves in the pit of his stomach and with those trembling hands. But something was keeping him from making his nerves work for him instead of against him. In the high-wire act Jones was expected to perform at Augusta National, something improvident had put a net underneath him. And that margin for error had nullified the genius that Jones had for golf. It had removed the element of danger that he had been able to overcome in his inimitable fashion and that had separated him from every other golfer in championships, national championships, at which he had once been six-to-five against the whole world.

With the Grand Slam, Bobby Jones had gone into golf's fourth dimension. He had been to some uncharted moon and back. Now that he was earthbound again, he just could not perform. Maybe the circumstances just weren't celestial enough. Whatever the reason, golf would have to do without him, and the game would never be the same. Men might hit longer and straighter shots, sink more putts, win more championships, even. In short, play better golf than Bobby Jones had.

But nobody would ever play *like* him.

With Jones never in contention, that inaugural tournament went along pretty much as might have been expected. Horton Smith, still at the peak of his game, stayed near or on top of the field all the way. Hard-hitting Craig Wood shot a 69 in the third round and then on the last day, playing just in front of Smith, posted a 71. But Smith, a very deliberate player with a methodical, almost surgical putting style, rolled in one of the twenty-footers he was becoming famous for to win by a stroke. A tall, handsome, courtly man, he would be congratulated by a number of ladies at Augusta National, one of whom was Alfred Bourne's daughter, whom he would eventually marry.

Horton Smith was the winner of the first and third Augusta National Invitation Tournaments.   Historic Golf Photos.

Smith would continue to play in The Masters until he could hardly walk, in his last year, 1963, when he knew he was dying from cancer. It was his way of saluting Bobby Jones, then very ill himself.

During the autumn of 1934, now that Augusta National had invited more members to join, it was found that play often had to be postponed in the morning so that frost would melt in the shadowy valleys where the first, second, third, and fourth greens then were. So the nines were reversed to Mackenzie's original routing. The switch would turn out to be a propitious one in ways nobody could foresee.

As architectural streamlines were made to the course over the years, the new back nine would become, while not necessarily more difficult to score on, infinitely more exciting to play and for galleries to watch the tournament, largely because of the absence of water hazards on the new front nine. What's more, a television camera aimed straight down the old eighteenth fairway from behind its green, which would now become the ninth hole, would have been shooting directly into the late-afternoon sun.

For the 1935 "Masters Tournament," once again Jones was reluctant to play. But now the economic argument was overwhelming. Season tickets had been only five dollars, two dollars for daily tournament rounds, and one dollar for practice rounds. So the first event had showed a sizable deficit, most of it due to the policy of accepting no volunteer help outside the membership. Prize money had been $5,000, the same as the Open Championship's. After receipts had been counted and local bills paid for tents, printing, sign making, and what not, Roberts had to pass the hat to meet the promised purse. Bart Arkell, who coincidentally owned that treasured collection of Dutch masters, put up the first prize of $1,500 and would continue to for some years, while Jay Monroe quietly committed himself to contributing second-place money.

As a man who had a hard time saying no to anybody about nearly anything, Jones had his headaches off the course as well as on.

Before the inaugural tournament, he had been swamped with requests for invitations to play, most of them from professionals, many of whom were obviously not of a caliber for the elite field he had in mind. A. G. Spalding & Bros. had put pressure on him to allow members of its vast pro staff to play. And Jones, as a Spalding vice president, felt duty bound to issue some of them invitations, although a number of them had scant reputation outside their own territories.

As a golfer who had won everything he had won while an amateur, Jones also did not want the tournament to become overwhelmingly a professional event, to degenerate into just another stop on the PGA tournament calendar. Something had to be done to perpetuate amateur golf throughout the world even though he would be absent from it. And this was, first and foremost, an invitational tournament. Consequently, he established a set of guidelines that would take the list of invitations out of his hands and settle once and for all who would be invited and who wouldn't. They would be:

- Present and past United States Open champions
- Present and past United States Amateur champions
- Present and past British Open champions
- Present and past British Amateur champions
- Present members of the United States Ryder Cup team
- Present members of the United States Walker Cup team
- Five professionals selected by the PGA for outstanding performance during the previous year
- Past winners of the PGA Championship (added in 1938)

If the first Augusta National Invitation had put itself inerasably into the record books unofficially as the "Masters

Tournament," the second would put it indelibly into golf's history by whatever name the press and therefore the public wanted to call it. To begin with, the field in 1935 was much stronger. Lawson Little had won both the United States and the British Amateur Championships in 1934 and would win both again this year, winning an unprecedented thirty-two straight matches before turning professional. He therefore qualified on two counts, giving the tournament some of the amateur flavor Jones was seeking.

Because he was playing so well on the tournament circuit, a young assistant pro from Ridgewood, New Jersey, by way of Texas, had been nominated by the PGA. His name was Byron Nelson, and he would be the front runner for a whole new brand of professional that would emerge from the Depression, not in spite of it but because of it.

Walter Hagen was back again. At forty-two, he was not quite over the hill. But he had won everything in golf it was possible to win at least twice: the United States Open, the British Open four times, and the PGA Championship a record five times, plus a string of tournaments so long even he had lost count. He would be the first golfer to earn $1,000,000, most of it through exhibitions.

Hagen notwithstanding, that year the top pro in the world had to be Gene Sarazen, born ten days after Jones to an immigrant carpenter from Italy. His real name was Saraceni, which he had discarded because he thought that it sounded too much like a violinist's. The shot Sarazen would bring off to win that 1935 "Masters" may not have been the greatest ever made, the luckiest, or even the most dramatic. But it was certainly the most readable combination of all three.

As major national championships had a way of evoking the heroic from Bobby Jones, his tournament at Augusta

National would prove to have a way of doing the same for others. While it may have been an exaggeration to say that Gene Sarazen hit "the shot heard round the world," as it was called then, that shot had a great deal to do with putting Augusta National on the tournament map and of making the public think that the Augusta National Invitation truly was "The Masters' Tournament."

Sarazen had come to the fifteenth tee in the fourth round needing three birdies on those final four holes to tie Craig Wood, who was already in the clubhouse with a 73 for a total of 282, six under par. In clubhouse terms, Sarazen had no chance. Paired with Hagen, Sarazen elected to go for the green at the par-five fifteenth, ignoring the water in front of it. Hagen smiled and shook his head. But if Sarazen were to get any birdies at all, one of them would have to be here. There were not more than a dozen spectators by the green, one of whom happened to be Bobby Jones, who had wandered down from the clubhouse out of curiosity, possibly because of the friendly rivalry between Sarazen and Hagen. It was an interesting pairing apart from the tournament, now that it was all but formally over.

Sarazen had started to choose his three-wood, but changed his mind to the four-wood before he pulled the three out of his bag. He then stepped into the shot with that one-piece swing of his, like a coach hitting fungoes to an outfielder. The ball struck the far bank of the water hazard abutting the green, skipped onto the putting surface, and softly rolled into the cup for a two. The odds on a double-eagle are approximately ten times higher than those for a hole-in-one, calling as it does for not one but two perfect shots, *if* the green is reachable to begin with. Professional and top amateurs who have made a dozen holes-in-one have never come close to making a double-eagle, so rare are they.

Whatever the actual odds were against the shot, with his double-eagle Sarazen had caught Wood on the card. He played the last three holes in pars to tie him. He then won, by five strokes, the thirty-six-hole play-off the following day, as usually happens to whoever causes a play-off any time in golf, perhaps out of sheer momentum.

Had Sarazen's shot won the United States Open or possibly even the British Open, it would still have had the same effect of near disbelief on the American public in 1935. Had it happened ten years later, probably not. Had it happened ten years earlier, certainly not. But it would be hard to choose a year in the country's history when Americans were more eager to accept the element of luck, not just in sports but in almost anything. (Even Charles Lindbergh was being referred to as "Lucky Lindy.") The nation had sunk to an emotional low point. It was without hope in the land of promise, without faith in the hard work that had made it so.

Having ridden high on laissez-faire capitalism throughout the twenties, the Crash of '29 had in six years left the United States in a state of economic chaos. One of every four working adults was out of work. Ten million other adults and an estimated 8,000,000 children were living on handouts and soup kitchens. Of the 7,000,000 citizens too old to work, not 200,000 of them had an income of any kind. All this was at a time when the population of the whole country was just 125,000,000.

To counteract the public mood, everything of an entertainment nature was plotted around the impossibly optimistic, not just the improbable. On the radio, Jack Benny could squeeze a dollar out of a nickel, Amos 'n' Andy a whole livelihood out of a broken-down taxi. In the movies, secretaries and waitresses who could hold a smile and tap dance without falling down somehow became stars of the Ziegfeld Follies overnight. As Tarzan, Johnny Weissmuller could out-swim a crocodile. In the newsreels, Babe Didrikson was running faster than men. And every now and then somebody tried to ride a barrel over Niagara Falls, just to get his picture in the tabloids.

The game of golf didn't have much to offer the man on the street, especially now that Bobby Jones was no longer performing the impossible. But it could offer up Eugene Saraceni, the son of an Italian immigrant, making a golf shot that was forty thousand to one. That it happened on Bobby Jones's golf course and during his tournament—well, there was hope yet, some things you could still have faith in. Sarazen's double-eagle didn't make the front pages, considering the aristocratic nature of golf and the threadbare condition of the public. But it came at a time when people would welcome anything lucky, anywhere they could find it, in the sports pages if they had to and about golf if they must, the closer to the impossible the better.

Gene Sarazen's double-eagle qualified as "impossible."

By 1936, nobody outside the Augusta National Golf Club was calling its tournament by any name other than the "Masters Tournament." But Bob Jones would not relent, and wouldn't for another two years. He still found the title embarrassing, and would continue to until he had stopped playing in the tournament.

In 1936, Horton Smith would become the first of a long line of two-time winners, chiefly by holing a fifty-foot chip across the undulated fourteenth green in a hard, cold rain in the last round. Smith was setting a precedent. Winning The Masters twice would in time become a new goal in golf for those who wanted to write part of its history. Not that you were a nobody by winning it once, but pros the public had never heard of before or since were now winning the United

States Open and the British Open. The public wanted new yardsticks for greatness.

By the end of that year, golf as a participant sport had fallen so far below the growth it had enjoyed in the twenties that there probably were not a thousand men in America who could break par on a first-rate course under any circumstances, much less a tournament, let alone a championship. But arising from the ashes of the Depression was a new kind of professional, and buried beneath it would be the old type of amateur, the kind who could play against the pros; like Ouimet, Travers, Evans, and, above all, Jones. Johnny Goodman in 1933 would be the last amateur to win a major Open Championship on either side of the Atlantic. And none would ever win a Masters Tournament.

All the truly great golf played in the future would be played by professionals, oddly enough not because of money but for the lack of it. After Lawson Little won both the United States and British Amateurs again in 1935, he could not afford even to try to defend his titles, and so grasped at the opportunity to play exhibitions for Spalding as a professional beginning in the spring of 1936.

The country was full of other young men nearly as, if not as, talented as Little who not only could not afford to play amateur golf but could not afford to play golf at all. While Little had been the son of an army officer stationed at San Francisco's Presidio, which had its own golf course, most of the others had picked up their golf as caddies and then sharpened it as shop assistants, a job that automatically took away their amateur standings. At that time, the USGA required a waiting period of up to six years before amateur status could be regained, during which time you could not play competitively as a pro *or* as an amateur.

The catch was, then, that the country's most talented players could not afford to play as amateurs and yet couldn't support themselves playing as professionals. Some of them grabbed what few club berths were to be had for young professionals. Some of them frittered away their talents at public links, which largely ignored the USGA. And some of them quit the game altogether.

But not all of them. A select few were possessed by the game. They didn't care under what circumstances they played so long as they could play competitively, so sure were they of their own talents. They worked at any job they could get at a private club during the summer months and then hit the tournament circuit in the winter, the circuit then consisting solely of a few standard events, such as the Los Angeles Open and the Texas Open, while the remainder were little more than conventions, during which manufacturers displayed their equipment for the coming season and then, to attract the pros, put up a few thousand dollars for a sideshow tournament. Out of friendship, most of those events were promoted by newspapermen, anxious for something to write about in the long months between football and baseball—January, February, March—professional basketball then being of little national interest and hockey only in the North.

Money or not, the talent was around, hidden in corners not theretofore known for their championship golfers, like Texas and West Virginia, and their names were Snead, Nelson, Demaret, and Hogan. "Believe it or not," Nelson would say of those early days, "I can't remember any of us talking about money. We just loved to play golf." If nothing else, they would prove that in golf quantity does not necessarily breed quality. Where today twelve thousand men in America make a living from theoretically being capable of breaking par, those four would break loose from the thousand men who couldn't break par under any circumstances. Together, they would rewrite the record books and establish a year-round PGA Tour worth millions in prize money. There were other such pros, to be sure. But those four alone would win ten of the next fifteen Masters Tournaments, not to mention everything else on the tournament and championship ledger.

When Gene Sarazen got his first look at Sam Snead, in 1936, his reaction would be typical in contemplating the future of the game now that hickory was part of its ancient past. Sarazen was paired with Snead during the third round of the Hershey Open, in Pennsylvania. After watching Snead hit one three-hundred-yard drive after another, splitting the seams of his shirts as he did so, Sarazen walked into the clubhouse and sat down at a table with pro Orville White. "I've just finished watching a kid who doesn't know the first thing about playing golf," Sarazen said, shaking his head. "But let me tell you something. I don't want to be around when he learns how."

The Age of Steel had arrived.

It is difficult for those golfers who have played with nothing but steel shafts to understand the improvements they made over hickory. Most think it was simply length, which actually had little or nothing to do with the difference. There were enormous hitters who used hickory shafts, although they were not as consistently long as the longest hitters are today with steel. The real difference in length would come from sophisticated improvements in the ball, not so much in the shaft. The technical difference was that steel eliminated torque in the shaft, allowing the clubface to return more nearly to the angle it had been placed in at the address. With hickory, you could never be sure. As the clubhead met the ball traveling at, say, a hundred-plus miles an hour and compressing it more than two hundred yards, a difference of half a degree could mean the difference between hitting that part of a green or fairway you were aiming at or missing it altogether.

But there was one enormous *physical* advantage steel had over hickory that the new breed of pros would use to its fullest. With steel, there was no end to how long you could practice. While Sam Snead might have become nearly the Sam Snead he became with hickory, what with his natural abilities, it's probably safe to say that Ben Hogan would not have become what he became had he not had steel shafts. For until Hogan came along, nobody ever shot 66s and *then* practiced, maybe for three hours. That doggedness is what separated Hogan from everybody before him, and most of those during his time. With hickory, Hogan would have worn out his shafts in a matter of weeks. And you don't win major national championships finding the feel of a new set of clubs every few months.

In the very first round of the 1937 "Masters," Byron Nelson would show the world just what sort of golf could be played with steel. Nelson hit every green in regulation figures except the four par-fives, which he hit in two, one less than regulation. Years before, Jones had played a round at Sunningdale, outside London, in what was widely heralded as the "perfect round," thirty-three shots and thirty-three pulls. But Nelson had played Augusta National in thirty-*two* shots.

Still, Nelson did not run away with the tournament. Hard on his heels was another steel-shaft wonder, Ralph Guldahl, who would be leading the tournament until he came to the twelfth and thirteenth holes, where he took a five and a six. Playing behind him, Nelson picked up six strokes on Guldahl by scoring a birdie-two and an eagle-three on the same holes, and went on to win by two strokes. "Amen Corner" had been discovered.

Byron Nelson, one of the first steel-shaft players, was one of the best golfers of the thirties. Historic Golf Photos.

Guldahl became one of golf's major mysteries. Of the new breed of pros that steel shafts were turning out, he was by far the most polished player. His consistency was so steady and his concentration so thorough that even Hogan was inspired by it, entertaining for the first time the notion that it was possible, if not probable, to play a round of golf without missing *any* shots. Having won the United States Open two months after Augusta, Guldahl would miss out again at Augusta by two strokes to Henry Picard in 1938. But he would take the 1939 event after his second Open Championship title in '38. Then, unexplainably, his game began to deteriorate. After the Second World War, he would continue to play in The Masters until 1973, when he was sixty-two. "What's that old guy doing out there?" a young pro asked a newspaperman who had watched Guldahl in his prime. "Why doesn't he make room for somebody who can win it?"

"Because," said the newspaperman, wistfully, "he thinks *he* can win it."

From 1939 on, the Augusta National Invitation would officially be known as The Masters Tournament. As it became increasingly apparent after 1934 that Bobby Jones was not going to win it, ticket sales began to slump, although Jones continued to draw by far the largest galleries.

Then in 1940 sales began to pick up. The event was getting tremendous advance publicity from another of the endless stream of pros pouring out of Texas: Nelson, Guldahl, Hogan, and now this one, Jimmy Demaret, a kind of latter-day Hagen. Handsome, all smiles, full of wisecracks, a man who would have a drink in his hands ten minutes after he finished his round, Demaret all but single-handedly changed the drab uniform of golf that for decades had been white broadcloth shirts, maybe with French cuffs, and neckties, both four-in-hands and bows. Some of the older pros were still wearing plus-fours.

Demaret would begin to wear purple slacks, fuchsia shirts, screaming argyles, and a Dutch baker-boy's cap with a pom-pom, looking one day like a pinball machine, the next like a jukebox. Despite his outrageous costumes and earthquake personality, he could play golf; there was no mistaking that. For six straight weeks before The Masters, Demaret had won each tournament on the circuit. By then, the public was beginning to learn how to pronounce his name, which wasn't DEM-ar-et or DEM-or-ay but De-MARE-it.

Texans monopolized the 1940 Masters, six of the top six-teen finishers having been born or raised there. Demaret set a new record for the dramatic back nine with a six-under 30, a new low for a major tournament. But the score was over-shadowed by another Texan, named Lloyd Mangrum, who established a new eighteen-hole record with a 64. Qualifying for the event as the PGA's nominee, Mangrum would nose out Nelson by a stroke, only to finish second. Playing just as he had for six weeks, Demaret won with ease for his seventh straight tournament. Then he went home to Houston, because, as he explained later, "I was afraid I might lose my job." He was assistant at River Oaks to pro-fessional Jack Burke, whose son would win The Masters six-teen years later.

Back in Houston, Demaret got a long-distance phone call from Ben Hogan, congratulating him for winning and thank-ing him, waggishly, for not coming to the tournament that Hogan was about to tee off in. It was the North-South Open in Pinehurst, North Carolina, being played over the Number Two Course that Donald Ross had revamped after his first look at Augusta National. Hogan so far had won only one tourna-ment, the Miami Four-ball, with Vic Ghezzi as his partner. But he would win this one by himself, and the next one the week after, and the third one the week after that. He would finish out the year as leading money-winner repeat in 1941, and lead again in 1942 before entering the Army Air Corps. One of the few things he unaccountably hadn't won by then was a Masters Tournament.

150

After Craig Wood finally won The Masters in 1941, topping off the year by winning the United States Open as well, Hogan tied for first with Nelson at Augusta in 1942. The play-off was an exhibition of steel-shaft golf at its professional best. After five holes, Hogan was leading by three strokes. He then played the next eleven holes in one under, only to watch Nelson play them in six under and go on to win by a stroke.

The public was at last aware that there was something to The Masters Tournament besides seeing who could beat Bobby Jones, although it was Jones whom the press wrote about the most before the tournament began and often clear up to the time it obviously was being won by others. Jones was still drawing the most enthusiastic galleries during the early rounds, even though he kept falling farther and farther behind the leaders. Hundreds of spectators even followed him in the final round, ignoring the winners altogether. And most newspapers carried something about Jones in their dispatches clear to the end.

Cliff Roberts thought that the press was distorting the nature of The Masters Tournament by reporting Jones's poor golf and saying less about the outstanding play that the new breed of pro was producing in the tournament. He collared Alan Gould, who reported golf for the Associated Press and who would later become the AP's executive editor. Gould listened patiently to Roberts's complaints, trying to take into consideration how little Roberts could know about journalism. Finally, he would take no more. "Look, Cliff," he said, "why don't you run the tournament and let me write about it? Bob Jones makes more news missing a putt than anybody else in the field does holing a brassie!"

Roberts would write later of the incident that Gould's bluntness "knocked the wind out of me." Knowing Jones personally as well as he then did, and seeing him almost daily for many weeks of the year, Roberts had simply been too close to him to realize the knight-errant that Jones still remained in the romance of American sports. In one strange sense, Jones was looming even larger as a folk figure than he had been when winning championships, in part because of his still early age. Since his retirement twelve years before, only Gene Sarazen had been able to win two major national championships in one year, a feat that Jones had pulled off three times in five years. And the Grand Slam was coming into focus for what it was, "the athletic achievement of the century," as it would be voted in two years by members of the AP, which included virtually every newspaper and newsmagazine in the country.

Jones was fast becoming a legend—more myth, actually, than man. A public up to its ears in defeatism wanted to read and to see for themselves that Bobby Jones was real, an actual person, and not some semifictional character from golf's gray and largely unwritten history that they had only heard about secondhand from old pros and fading amateurs in locker rooms and golf shops.

The Masters Tournament at Augusta National was the only demonstrable proof still left them. In time, Roberts would give the press the finest facilities in sports, complete with binoculars to read a scoreboard that wasn't fifty feet away, private interview rooms, and eventually television sets that carried tournament proceedings over a closed circuit. If he knew the course well enough, a reporter could passably if not intelligently cover a Masters Tournament without leaving press headquarters. Some did.

CHAPTER 9:
SECOND WORLD WAR

T he Second World War made national golf championships seem competitively puny and somehow
unpatriotic, so the United States Golf Association
suspended both its Amateur and Open Championships for the
duration. President Roosevelt had publicly announced that he
thought a continuation of professional baseball and football
would be good for the morale of both troops and the home
front, and so, taking this cue, the PGA kept its golf circuit
going, despite gas rationing and other restrictions on travel.

Sam Snead had a business manager named Fred
Corcoran, a Boston Irishman with an encyclopedic knowledge of tournament golf who, as a friend of Jones's also, had
become a sideline fixture at The Masters Tournament,
where he could usually be found hanging out at press headquarters, giving newspapermen, whose company he enjoyed,
an endless spiel of anecdotes interlaced with historical facts
and statistics not available in golf's then sketchy record
books. Corcoran knew what made the tournament circuit go
round, and he had a first-name relationship with seemingly
half the pros in America.

With the PGA's blessing, Corcoran put a patchwork tournament schedule together, although he had few famous pros to peddle to potential sponsors. Snead would enlist in the navy along with Demaret, Hogan would enlist in the Army Air Corps, and Lloyd Mangrum would become an infantryman in the European Theater, where he would be awarded two Purple Hearts for wounds in battle. So Corcoran made do with what he had: older, married pros, most of whom had been talented enough to play in The Masters, such as Craig Wood, Jug McSpaden, Toney Penna, even Tommy Armour now and then, and Sam Byrd, who had switched to pro golf after playing as a substitute outfielder for the New York Yankees.

Corcoran had a huge drawing card, though, in Byron Nelson, excused from military duty because he had a blood-clotting condition, although not hemophilia, as the public erroneously thought. Fortunately for golf, Nelson was one of those rare players, in the manner of Jones, who often did not need much competition to bring forth their best golf. Some of the scores Nelson would shoot during the war years, as the troops would read, must have had to be seen to be believed. And they were. Snead and Hogan, for two, couldn't wait to get back on a tournament circuit where you had to score in the 60s just to survive.

In a matter of weeks after Pearl Harbor, Augusta became the total military town. It already had five army installations, among them Camp Gordon. (Later changed to Fort Gordon.) But numerous others were jerry-built on the periphery of Augusta, making travel to and from the city by civilians something they would just as soon not do. Out of a uniform, men felt frowned upon on a train or an airliner. In a car—well, gas was being meted out with government stamps, and nine-tenths of Augusta National's members who were not in the service themselves lived too many stamps away.

Jones and Roberts decided immediately after the 1942 Masters Tournament to close down the entire club for the duration, even to the point of suspending dues. Members were asked, instead, to contribute $100 a year for taxes, a caretaker's salary, and basic maintenance. The clubhouse staff, which had never been large to begin with, was dismissed, and so were the grounds staff, with the exception of Simk Hammack, who had been the club's greenkeeper since its beginning. Hammack told Roberts that he had previous experience in raising turkeys, and he thought he could do so profitably on the grounds during the war, when they would be badly needed for food, anyway. Roberts shrugged his shoulders, and said go ahead. The club had nothing to lose. Two hundred head of steers had been purchased to keep the grass mowed, and that's all that would be on the property until the war ended.

There was no keeping Bobby Jones out of uniform. He was too competitive to stand on the sidelines, for one thing. For another, he did not have to be told that the armed services wanted all the nationally celebrated figures they could possibly recruit, especially from sports, to make the war effort appear in the newspapers as near total as it could get. But, for numerous reasons, Jones was technically ineligible for military duty.

To begin with, he was forty years old, way beyond draft age then, and had no military experience of any nature, not even college ROTC. He had a wife and now three children, giving him four more exemptions. And, finally, he was medically classified as "4-F," meaning he had a physical disability, in his case a serious varicose-vein condition that had once required not altogether successful surgery. He used that condition to explain to authorities that he could not spend this war, as he had the last, raising money for the Red Cross or for War Bonds

Jones in uniform for the Army Air Corps. AP/Wide World Photos.

by playing a long series of exhibitions. His legs couldn't take the strain.

That may have been the only lie the George Washington of golf ever told. How could a man incapable of walking four and a half miles around a golf course be capable of fighting a war?

Jones pleaded his case to the Army Air Corps, as though service in that branch would excuse him from walking. (Certainly, at his age, he did not expect to be taught how to fly.) Recruitment officers did not want to lose this superhero who was standing before them, volunteering. So they winked, knowing they could bind Jones to a desk somewhere and make use of a first-rate analytic mind in their intelligence branch.

Jones was commissioned a captain immediately after the 1942 Masters Tournament and sent to Harrisburg, Pennsylvania, for ten weeks of intensified training in aerial-photo interpretation, air navigation, and saturation-bombing tactics and techniques. Then, by the twists of logic the military mind often makes in the midst of war, he was afterward assigned to interrogating German prisoners of war, undoubtedly because he was an attorney, although he could not speak German and had only a scant reading knowledge of it. Years later, he would say to a friend, with a wry smile, "I think that I made the mistake of telling some colonel over a drink that I had once read Goethe. He thought I meant in German. It was in English."

Jones would be asked just once more to help raise money for a war effort with his golf game. In June of 1942, with the Chicago District Golf Association and the PGA as cosponsors, the USGA staged an ersatz Open Championship at Chicago's Ridgemoor Country Club. It was called the Hale America National Open Golf Tournament, the USGA carefully avoiding the word "championship," which the public overlooked. It also misinterpreted the word "Hale" euphonically to mean "Hail," when in fact Hale was the name of a Ridgemoor member who had suggested the tournament as a way of raising money for the Navy Relief Society and the United Service Organization, which operated hospitality centers for troops throughout the world and produced entertainment for them.

Jones played in khaki, the only man in the field who did with the exception of Sgt. Jim Turnesa, of the famous Turnesa brothers. Jones got a thundering ovation when he stepped to the first tee, and he did not let the gallery down, scoring a two-under-par 70, although he had not had a club in his hands for ten weeks. He finished out the event, as weakly as only he expected, with a score of 290, two over par, while Ben Hogan ran away with the tournament, scoring a 62 in the second round to win eventually with a 271. Jones then went back to war.

All Jones's superior officers clear up to the Pentagon of course knew who he was. He badgered enough of them until he finally got the overseas duty he wanted. Promoted to major, he was stationed in northwestern England with the Ninth Air Corps, which in the spring of 1944 came directly under the command of General Dwight Eisenhower, whose headquarters were in England. Jones and Eisenhower might have had a chance to meet but never did, not surprisingly considering the vast differences in rank and responsibilities. Eisenhower's favorite game was golf, although he had been only a sporadic player at best. But the fame of each would eventually bring them together.

On D-Day plus One—June 7, 1944—Jones and the unit under his command, now temporarily converted to much-needed infantry, hit the beachhead at Normandy, spending two days and nights under artillery fire. After a few months near the front lines, when Allied supremacy had become obvious, Jones was mustered out as a lieutenant colonel.

Jones would afterward speak little about his war experiences, scoffing at them if he did mention them at all, just as he would begin to about the golf wars he had been in. When you now brought up the subject of the Grand Slam, as such, he would change the conversation or turn enigmatically silent, shrug his shoulders if you persisted, or cut you off altogether by staring philosophically out a window. The Grand Slam was becoming part of golf's unread history. Jones was content to let it lie.

After returning home from service in Europe in the late fall of 1944, now that an Allied victory was a certainty, Jones and Roberts agreed that they ought to open up the club the next year. The course was in pathetic shape. The steers put out to pasture two years before had not only eaten the turf, plus an expensive amount of feed when the Bermuda grass went dormant, they had also chewed away a lot of the flowering shrubs and the bark off many irreplaceable trees. Much to Jones and Roberts's surprise, Simk Hammack's turkey farm had turned a profit of $5,000, enabling the club to offset much of the damage the steers had done. With skilled and even unskilled labor practically nonexistent, forty-two German prisoners of war incarcerated at Camp Gordon were hired and paid for six months, with army permission, to put Augusta National back in prewar shape.

During the war, the Bon Air had fallen out of the Vanderbilt chain, changing ownership several times, with the result that it no longer offered the deluxe services it had under Walton Marshall. Among other special touches by Marshall, the Bon Air had staged a black-tie dance the night before each Masters Tournament for Augusta National members, Masters contestants, and local dignitaries, the gala preceded that afternoon by a grand parade downtown on Broad Street. The party was called The Golf Ball. What else?

With Augusta National's membership now standing at 149, only 30 of whom lived in Augusta, Jones and Roberts somehow had to find accommodations to replace the Bon Air, falling to seed as it was. Some of the *intime* that had set Augusta National apart from the impersonal country clubs in

America's suburbs would have to be sacrificed. Rooms would have to be added somehow, the old manor house having nothing more than what amounted to a dormitory in its cupola.

Neither Jones nor the financially savvy Roberts knew at those uncertain times how to underwrite such a project. But once again one of the club's powerhouse members stepped forward to hold together this club that so many of them had grown to love as an old-shoe retreat from the starchy worlds of commerce and finance. A New York member named Edward J. Barber, who ran the Barber Steamship Lines, put forth a complex underwriting plan that would allow the club to go ahead with the construction of a new wing, which would include another dining room and new kitchen, five suites in another wing, and a number of bedrooms. There would also be two cottages, one for Jones himself right next to the tenth tee, so he could see the action in The Masters without having to shake hands like a ward heeler, awkwardly autograph golf balls, and feign laughter at golf stories he had heard a hundred times before.

The building project, to be expanded even more in later years, cost Barber $25,000 out of his own pocket immediately and another $200,000 from his will, eventually. More importantly, the plan was the catalyst for many more financial gifts that would make the more expansive Augusta National what it is today.

It has often been said that The Masters Tournament *is* The Masters Tournament in large part because it is played at the same site every year, Augusta National, as though the club had always been there, full blown in some Zeus-like manner off Bobby Jones's forehead. But few people knew how often Augusta National came close to ceasing to be a golf club at all, and would have had it not been for generous members who found in the club that which they most liked about a golf club.

Long before he was famous, Bobby Jones had a way of looking at the world from high above, like an eagle, viewing life in the grand manner. Cliff Roberts, on the other hand, reveled in ground-level details, at which he was a master, often implementing Jones's ambitious ideas to tiny degrees that Jones had not the patience for. With a man of Jones's stature behind him, Roberts could fill the role, with often exasperating precision, of a full-feathered chief among a lot of very big Indians.

Still, Roberts wasn't a financial magician, for all his reputation on Wall Street. He couldn't pull cash out of a hat, as though it were a rabbit. He had to get the money somewhere, and that somewhere had to be the membership in those days before The Masters Tournament became big business. To compound the problem, Augusta National as a golf club, pure and simple, was hardly looked upon as a charity by the Internal Revenue Service. So the club grew nearly to what it is today, and The Masters Tournament along with it, largely because of gifts that were in no sense tax write-offs. Most of these sometimes anonymous gifts were made by early members unknown today.

By summer of 1945, Jones and Roberts saw no reason not to start up The Masters Tournament again in 1946. The course would be ready, the members were eager, and there was a fantastic brand of golf being played on the PGA tournament circuit.

Discharged from the navy because of a back injury, Snead had won the very first tournament of 1945, the Los Angeles Open, and would win five other events before the year was over, although a broken bone in his wrist put him out of action for the summer. Hogan, discharged from the Army Air Corps, was back on the trail by late summer and would win five tournaments. But Nelson would win *nineteen*, eleven of them in a row, although the record books today cut Nelson's string off at eighteen. (A tournament that he won in Spring Lake, New Jersey, was at first canceled, then played anyway, and somehow in the confusion got lost in the PGA's catch-as-catch-can archives.) Confusing 1945 with the year before, when Nelson also won practically every tournament he entered, some bar-stool historians would say years later that Nelson won what he won because he didn't have to beat anybody. And he didn't— if you regarded Sam Snead and Ben Hogan as nobodies.

The first postwar Masters Tournament was expected to be a show of Nelson against the field. It wasn't. Nelson was dog-tired. He had, in fact, passed up numerous events in 1945, pleading exhaustion, having spent three straight years travel-ing coast to coast and border to border by car with his wife, Louise. Barely thirty-four, he announced early in 1946 that he would play in no more national championships after that year's United States Open (which he eventually lost in a play-off to Lloyd Mangrum), limiting his tournament appearances to The Masters and to his friend Bing Crosby's Pro-Am at Pebble Beach. Although he would never win another Masters, he was a factor for several years. In 1951, playing hardly any golf at all, he hit the headlines one last time by winning The Crosby—the pro part, not the pro-am.

The 1946 Masters Tournament was one of the oddest ever played. You could have looked at it in two ways. Either a jour-neyman pro named Herman Keiser led all the way, or Ben Hogan couldn't quite catch him. Having been five strokes behind Keiser after the first round, seven behind after the sec-ond, Hogan found himself on the eighteenth green of the last round needing to force a play-off only two putts from twelve feet above the hole, nearly the same spot from which Keiser himself had just three-putted. So did Hogan.

"That first putt of mine rolled so slowly toward the hole, I swear I could read the print on it," Hogan would recall years later. "Then it broke right, three feet past, meaning it would have to break left coming back. But it didn't. It broke right again. I was told that the next day half a dozen members tried to make the same putt, and all of them missed on the right. That summer they resurfaced that part of the green."

While that resurfacing was only minor, there would be innumerable other changes made to Augusta National all but invisibly, sometimes so subtly that even members didn't notice the changes from one season to another. There were alterations that were obvious, too, all of which would leave Augusta National in a constant state of improvement that continues to this day. Most of the original changes had been suggested by contestants, particularly by past winners, and usually at a special dinner for them begun in 1953 at the suggestion of Ben Hogan and held in the clubhouse the Tuesday night before the tournament itself begins.

Until his death, all those changes had to be funneled through Bobby Jones. There had been hundreds of them, and Jones rejected all except those that he thought would genuinely improve the shot values of the course without making it unduly hazardous for the members, who some well-intentioned pros thought didn't exist, so unobtrusively did all of them act while The Masters was going on. Augusta National members didn't have to throw any weight around during the week of The Masters. They had Cliff Roberts to do that for them.

Two major changes had been made before the war. In 1937, the green for the tenth hole was moved atop a hill behind its location then, away from a valley that couldn't drain well enough for a putting surface and which, besides, made the hole too short. A bunker that had guarded the left side and part of the green's rear was enlarged, like some gigantic amoeba, solely to break up the monotony of the fairway as it swept up to the new green. The bunker was thought to be more decorative than hazardous, sitting as it does nearly four hundred yards from the tee and, yet, way short of the green. Then, in a Masters Tournament during the late seventies, pro Tom Weiskopf *drove* into it, proving a pet theory of Jones that no matter where you locate a bunker, somebody will someday find a way of getting into it somehow.

The second major alteration had been made on the seventh hole in 1938 at the suggestion of Horton Smith. Like the old tenth, that hole also had been too short. Smith proposed that a postage-stamp green, surrounded by bunkers, be relocated atop the hill behind it. Lacking distinction until then, the seventh became an uncommonly difficult short par-four, a type of hole all too rare in golf, architecturally difficult as it is to conceive, keeping it small and still functional, like a two-room house. Some players in The Masters found that a pitch not quite bold enough to reach the flagstick would suck back into a bunker. Some who had been too bold, thereby leaving themselves with a putt from above the hole, watched haplessly while their putts rolled into the very bunker they had been trying to avoid with their pitches.

The par-three sixteenth hole, only 110 yards long, had been an enjoyable one for the members, but it was being torn to shreds by the pros. In 1947, Jones had been helping found a new club in Atlanta to be called Peachtree. By the purest of coincidences, the architect he employed was named Robert T. Jones, the *T* standing for "Trent," which everybody who knew both Joneses called him to distinguish one from the other as Trent grew famous in his own right. Bob Jones consulted Trent Jones about the sixteenth at Augusta National.

Trent's ambitious plan would make the sixteenth much longer, move it farther away from the fifteenth green, add a larger water hazard, and make it altogether one of the more exciting holes for the gallery. Cliff Roberts was offended, for some curious reason, that he had not been more closely consulted about the changes. At about this stage in Augusta National, he was patently beginning to regard himself as Bobby Jones's alter ego. He would persist in saying that the new sixteenth was entirely Bob Jones's design, when, in truth, it was Trent Jones's as approved by Bob.

On and on the improvements would go, the eleventh to have its tee moved seventy yards to the left, thereby removing a dogleg that made some contestants lay up off the tee with an iron. Water from Rae's Creek was dammed to form a lake to the left-front of the green. Added to the already famous thirteenth and the par-three twelfth, which Hogan had said was the toughest hole on the entire course, the more muscular eleventh made Amen Corner even more prayerful than it already was. Trent Jones was chiefly responsible for this change in the course, too, again with Bob Jones's consultation and approval. But Roberts would go on to say, this time, that the scheme was his. Both Joneses shrugged their shoulders and said nothing.

The year 1948 would turn out to be one of the most momentous in Augusta National's history. To start with, The Masters Tournament held expectations of being a free-for-all among the steel-shaft superstars. Hogan was on his way to becoming leading money-winner on the tournament circuit for the fifth time, a rested Nelson was presumed to still have some greatness left in him, Mangrum had put a United States Open under his belt, a South African oddity named Bobby Locke was confounding the American pros by winning with a figure-eight in his back-swing, Demaret had won his second Masters the year before and was telling the press that it was a better tournament than the Open Championship, and Snead was—well, Sam Snead. What more need you ask?

But the tournament turned out to be no fight at all, let alone a free-for-all. It was won by five strokes, with a record-tying score of 279, by Claude Harmon, who the public thought was nothing more than a club pro playing out a hot hand. Harmon was a club pro, all right. One of his clubs was Winged Foot, where Jones had won the Open Championship in 1929. Harmon had shot Winged Foot once in 62. In the winters, his other club was Seminole, near Palm Beach, a masterpiece by Donald Ross. Harmon had once shot *it* in an even 60.

Just before going to Augusta for The Masters, Harmon had been playing almost daily at Seminole with his old friend Hogan, "beating him as often as he did me," as Harmon would recall. "When I began the last nine holes with a five-shot lead at Augusta," Harmon went on, "I told myself that if I couldn't win this tournament I was in the wrong business."

Almost immediately after that Masters Tournament, Augusta National would be visited by General Eisenhower, taking his first vacation in ten years. The visit would have much to do with his becoming President of the United States four years later.

That 1948 Masters Tournament would be the last golf Bobby Jones would ever play. Although he said nothing, something in his right hand and shoulder was bothering him. He chalked it up to age. At forty-six, his hair was thinning and he had a slight paunch. Playing in the same old broad-cloth shirt from the style of his day, although now without the necktie, he wore brown brogues, no cap, no glove, and dark brown trousers that looked like half of a suit and had a long key chain draped from the belt to the right pocket. If you didn't know who he was, as he stood nonchalantly by a tee, you might have thought him a member who had somehow wormed his way into the tournament.

You might, that is, until it was his turn to play. Then, if you still didn't understand who he was, you knew as soon as he went into his swing that he had to be somebody special, old-fashioned key chain and all.

It was that touch of poetry. The beauty of him somehow came across without your having to understand who he was.

CHAPTER 10:
GENERAL
EISENHOWER

I n 1948, William E. Robinson, an Augusta National member, was general manager of the *New York Herald Tribune*, and later became its publisher. The year before, he had been instrumental in convincing General Eisenhower that he should write his military memoirs, which were eventually published in book form by Doubleday & Company and serialized in Robinson's newspaper, which was the quasi-official voice of the Republican party in the East.

A robust, extroverted Irishman, ten years younger than Eisenhower, Robinson became an immediate friend of the General's. When, early in 1948, Eisenhower finished his memoirs, *Crusade in Europe*, Robinson invited him to Augusta National for a holiday, the first vacation he would have in ten years. Eisenhower arrived on April 13. The streets of Augusta were lined with cheering crowds clear to the club all the long way from the airport. General and Mrs. Eisenhower stayed eleven days in Bobby Jones's cottage.

While at the club, Eisenhower met a group of members whom he would soon label "the gang." He found that he could relax with them as he could with no other civilians, and they would remain his closest friends outside the military for the rest of his life. They would, in historical fact, guide his career from then on.

Robinson became not only Eisenhower's closest friend but also the man who would lead him through the political labyrinth that eventually ended in his election as President. Cliff Roberts invested the $500,000 that the General realized after taxes from *Crusade*, which gave him the financial security he deserved, no mean feat, since the General had returned from Europe broke.

Two other members of "the gang" were Bob Woodruff, chairman of the board of Coca-Cola, and W. Alton "Pete" Jones, president of Cities Service Company, who had a rags-to-riches career that had left him enormously wealthy and carefree about cash. (After Jones was killed in a 1962 airline accident and $60,000 was found in his pocket, Roberts would recall that Jones, over Roberts's admonitions, had never gone anywhere without at least one $10,000 bill in his wallet, just so he could have the satisfaction of knowing he could buy almost anything he liked on the spur of the moment.) When Eisenhower announced three years later that he would run for the presidency, Pete Jones offered to help finance his campaign to the tune of $1,000,000. A much smaller sum was actually accepted.

A fourth member of "the gang" was Ellis "Slats" Slater, in whose suite would be discovered, in 1983, the original sketch for Augusta National drawn by Alister Mackenzie. Slater was president of Frankfort Distilleries. His wife, Priscilla, would become Mamie Eisenhower's closest friend.

The fifth member of the group was George Allen, who had already met the General during the war. The only Democrat among them, Allen was then privy to President Truman, had also been close to Roosevelt, and would be to a number of others yet to occupy the White House, prompting him later to write a tongue-in-cheek book, *Presidents Who Have Known Me*. A powerful corporate lawyer in both Washington and New York, Allen was a near-professional comic, especially with the anecdotal belly laugh, usually aimed at himself. He was one of the few persons who could keep the usually restrained Eisenhower doubled over with laughter. It was Allen who would find the farm at Gettysburg, Pennsylvania, to which the Eisenhowers would later retire. To ensure their privacy, Allen bought up all the farmland that surrounded it.

During his stay, the General played golf every day and took a number of lessons from Ed Dudley. Eisenhower was not a good golfer, seldom breaking 95, in part because of a trick left knee from his football days that made it hard for him to shift his weight and follow through properly. But golf was by far his favorite game, followed closely by bridge, at which he was nearly an expert. At Augusta National he was pleased to find partners, notably in Cliff Roberts, to whom he did not have to explain the finer points of the game. Later, he would import partners and opponents of his own, notably Gen. Alfred Gruenther, an internationally recognized authority on the rules of bridge.

Much to Jones's and Roberts's surprise, Eisenhower asked while at Augusta National if he might join the club, ordinarily a sure way of never becoming a member. They were delighted, of course, but nevertheless stuck to a provision established when the club had been started that there would never be any honorary memberships, not even now for a general of the army who had successfully led the largest military campaign in the history of warfare. Eisenhower understood, and was more than happy to become a dues-paying member.

General Eisenhower prepares for a friendly game with Arnold Palmer and Clifford Roberts. Historic Golf Photos.

Throughout the uproar over Eisenhower's first visit, and through all the subsequent ones, Jones remained in the background, quietly indulgent toward the undisguised hero-worship his members were quite naturally displaying over the General. He knew what the situation was like that Eisenhower was in, having once been put on such a pedestal himself.

But there were other reasons why Jones kept his reserve. He was apolitical, and so was bored by the political talk that dragged far into the nights, particularly since Eisenhower himself wasn't sure whether he was a Democrat or a Republican. When Eisenhower finally ran on the Republican ticket, Jones would vote for him and even go so far as to appear on television in his behalf. But he did so, apart from friendship, only because he thought it time the South stopped voting solidly Democratic and began a two-party system.

Also, Jones did not play bridge. Indoor games just did not have the appeal for him of outdoor games, such as baseball, with its endless strategies that had to be carried out or thwarted physically. He found chess, checkers, and even crossword puzzles crashing bores. Jones liked to have his mind enlightened, not just entertained; his wits stretched, not just tested. The sort of puzzles he liked to solve were more likely to be found in books and records, of which by now he had put together considerable collections. Why did Melville allow saintly Billy Budd to be hanged from a yardarm? Why did Mozart have Don Giovanni refuse to relent over his decadence? These were the sorts of problems that Bobby Jones thought were worth trying to solve, perhaps because they were insoluble.

Purely for social reasons, however, Jones taught himself how to play bridge. He read every book on the game he could lay his hands on. When he began to play, hesitantly at first, he impressed everybody, even General Gruenther, with his knowledge. But he never learned to play the game with much savoir-faire, mainly because he played too much "by the book" while his more experienced opponents played less conventionally.

There was a further, more serious, reason why Jones remained apart from the Eisenhower golf and bridge games and all the political side talk that went with them. He was becoming increasingly concerned about his health. He had suffered painful cricks in his neck and severe back spasms dating from 1926. But he knew, instinctively, that this time they were more serious. Bobby Jones was a very sick man, far more sick than he imagined; far more, in truth, than his doctors first guessed. It would take them eight years to diagnose what was actually wrong with him.

Obviously, there was something the matter with Jones's spine. His legs were weakening—the right one, in fact, was noticeably dragging—and there was notable atrophy in his right arm. He told his doctors in Atlanta that on at least two occasions that he could remember from his championship days he had felt as though he had wrenched his back, which he attributed to the pronounced pivot he took and for which he was so admired among the pros, turning on the ball, as he did, with his feet barely separated, even on a full drive.

X-rays indicated an abnormal bone growth on three cervical vertebrae. The condition was operable but extremely dangerous. It had been performed no more than fourteen times in the United States at that time. If unsuccessful, it could paralyze the patient from the neck down. Jones told the surgeons to go ahead. He preferred the risk to living as a cripple.

The operation was performed in November of 1948 at Emory University Hospital, in Atlanta. It was successful; or, more accurately, not unsuccessful. Jones was not paralyzed, but the condition was not alleviated. Instead, it grew steadily worse. Over the next two years, the atrophy began to spread to the left side of his body as well.

This time the condition was thought due to a damaged disc that was pressing against a nerve. Jones underwent a second operation at the Lahey Clinic, in Boston, in May of 1950. A team of surgeons removed some flesh, thereby hoping to make Jones more comfortable. But beyond that, they knew there was nothing further they could do. Jones's nervous system was permanently damaged in the upper regions of his spine. He would experience gradual deterioration of the nerves below that point for the remainder of his life. It would be physical torture. By way of relieving the mental torture that would go with it, they stressed that none of the damage had been caused by the first operation. He was not to think that, if it were any consolation. Which it wasn't.

In the following six years, Jones went from a cane to a leg brace, then to crutches and braces on both legs. The pain was nearly unbearable at times, eased temporarily only by doses of codeine. Early in 1956, his personal physician in Atlanta, Dr. Frank M. Atkins, suggested that he be examined at Columbia-Presbyterian Medical Center, in New York City, by Dr. H. Houston Merritt, who had become interested in his case.

Dr. Merritt was dean of the College of Physicians and Surgeons at Columbia-Presbyterian and chairman of its Department of Neurology. He was internationally recognized in medicine, notably for having been the first to use the drug Dilantin in treating epilepsy.

Jones spent five days being examined by Dr. Merritt at Columbia-Presbyterian, and was released on July 13. Shortly thereafter, Dr. Merritt filed a two-and-a-half-page report on Jones and what was wrong with him. He concluded that Jones was suffering from an extremely rare disease medically known as syringomyelia.

Back in 1941, the New York Yankees great first baseman, Lou Gehrig, had died from a rare spinal disease called amyotrophic lateral sclerosis, which became known by the public thereafter as "Lou Gehrig's disease." There would be no convenient label for what Bobby Jones had. It was almost as rare as Jones himself. Neurosurgeons who had treated maybe a dozen cases of "Lou Gehrig's disease" might spend their entire careers only reading about syringomyelia.

The disease is thought to be congenital, which is to say Jones's doctors thought he had been born with it. But it is not hereditary; Jones had not inherited it and neither would his children. There is no known cure for it, not even a universally accepted treatment. In simplified terms, fissures, or small cavities, had developed in Jones's central nervous system, thereby short-circuiting the commands his brain was giving to his motor nerves. In the early stages, Jones had noticed that his fingers would not grasp things until a split second after he thought they would. As the motor nerves became more and more damaged, muscular atrophy set in, permitting the body to waste away. Eventually, Jones would have no feeling below his waist but, paradoxically, a deep, unceasing ache in his neck and upper arms.

Syringomyelia does not affect vision, hearing, or thinking. Jones would remain perfectly lucid, even alert, for the rest of his days. But the cruelest of all possible blows was that the disease does not kill its victims. They simply die from exhausting side effects, possibly a heart attack in some form. The process can be very slow, but had not been heard of to last more than fifteen years from its first symptoms. Jones would confound medicine by living twenty-three years.

In the early days, before he knew what actually was wrong with him, Jones tried to fight the disease. In the middle of the night, once, Jones had wakened from a deep sleep to go to the bathroom. Forgetting that he could hardly walk, he slipped out of bed and fell flat on his face, unable to right himself for ten minutes. He just lay there, swearing every profanity he could think of while beating his fists on the floor.

After syringomyelia had been explained by Dr. Merritt, Jones came to accept the disease philosophically, as only a man might who could weigh in his mind the incongruous, imponderable fates of a Billy Budd and a Don Giovanni. What was meant to be was meant to be, and so Jones forced himself to accept his burden with all the grace he could muster. He refused to act any more disabled than he had to. The public never knew what was wrong with him. Rumor had it that he had some rare form of arthritis, and that's what the public persisted in believing. "Let's just let it go at that," Jones said to a writer-friend after explaining syringomyelia. "It's easier to understand."

For nearly ten more years, Jones went to his office in downtown Atlanta from his home in suburban Druid Hills almost every working day, driven there by a chauffeur, who would then lift him into a collapsible wheelchair and push him to his office. Jean Marshall, his private secretary, would arrange a row of cigarettes in holders for him, these to protect him from burning his fingers, since he couldn't feel the heat. A lighter that would flick on at just a touch was set beside them. In time, he got so he couldn't work that, and the cigarettes had to be lighted for him. A chain-smoker since his college days, he left a friend speechless at this time by saying that he was going to give them up someday. Jones had not lost his capacity for looking into the future, grim though it was.

Jean Marshall had arranged a fountain pen wrapped in a rubber ball so Jones could grasp it, and thus he continued his lifelong practice of answering all letters by return mail and personally signing them, although by now he could no longer manage the old autograph, "Robt. T. Jones, Jr." He just wrote "Bob Jones" or "Bob" in a huge, halting scroll, as a child would learning the alphabet. Telephone calls were answered through a desktop speaker, and he spoke to everyone with a cheerfulness that set each of them aback. Eventually, he could not move around at all without his wheeled walker. Even then, he required round-the-clock male nurses, muscular young men who could handle him, as Jones would say with a chuckle, "like a flap-jack."

Jones by now could only listen to music when somebody played the records for him, of course. But he slowly began to find the phonograph a bother. He had long ceased to play bridge, because he could no longer hold the cards. Reading had become a chore, because he could no longer turn the pages. When a friend in New York found a machine at Hammacher Schlemmer that would hold a book and all but turn the pages for him, Jones declined the gift. "The hell with it," he told the man on the phone. "The truth is, I can't keep my mind on what I'm reading."

In spite of his condition, Jones managed to turn out two more books, by dictation, an effort that can still only be described as Herculean. The first book was a disjointed memoir, entitled *Golf Is My Game*. The other was that collection of his best instructional columns, *Bobby Jones on Golf*. He had been persuaded to put the books together mainly because they would certainly end up on library shelves, where the generations after he was gone could read what he thought about golf To his surprise, he earned in the neighborhood of $50,000 in royalties from them. He thought the public had forgotten about him. In any event, he was delighted to make extra money from golf at this stage in his life. Although his income from his law practice and business interests was more than adequate—indeed, he had set up a substantial trust fund for his wife and children—he thought golfers no longer cared what he thought about the game. Besides, any unexpected income was always useful. His medical bills were now running into the tens of thousands of dollars.

Throughout his suffering, Jones continued to go to every Masters Tournament. For a while, he ventured out in a golf cart, driven by a member, such as Charley Yates, a happy-go-lucky Atlantan who had won the British Amateur in 1938, had then become an Augusta National member, and would eventually succeed Fielding Wallace as the club's secretary. During The Masters, Yates took on one of the most harried jobs a member could be asked to perform, running the pressroom.

When Jones could no longer ride in a cart, he sat in his cottage, holding court for old friends among the pros, such as Fred McLeod, who had won the United States Open in 1908, and Jock Hutchison, who had won the British Open in 1921.

For many years, McLeod and Hutchison served as honorary starters at The Masters, playing nine holes just in front of the field itself. They continued to play together until 1973, when Hutchison was eighty-eight and McLeod two years older. Hutchison had to drop out thereafter because of an ailing hip, but McLeod continued playing alone for three more years. The custom had brought the golf-wise galleries at Augusta to its feet in applause on every hole. After Hutchison dropped out, McLeod was asked why he continued playing alone. He took a sip from the nipper of scotch he liked to nurse and said, in all seriousness, "Jock was getting too damn old. I wasn't."

In the sixties, Jones would make only one appearance a year before the public. This would be on the lawn between Prosper Berckmans's old manor house and the course itself, where immediately after The Masters Tournament the winner would be inducted ceremonially into the club by putting on the green jacket emblematic of an Augusta National member. It was tailored especially for the club by the Brooks Uniform Company, in New York City, using a material in a distinctive shade of forest green that the Brooks people set aside exclusively for the club's use. The jacket was to be worn by members only on Augusta National's premises. Wearing it elsewhere could cost one his membership, which he would know he had lost when he stopped getting bills in the mail. That was part of Cliff Roberts's silent treatment.

The green jacket became Augusta National's, and hence The Masters's, coat of arms, so unmistakably that it became both the club's and the tournament's semiofficial symbol. (A restaurant directly across the street, much to the club's dismay, would name itself the Green Jacket, and a facsimile of the jacket would be used commercially all over the city year-round by dry cleaners, auto laundries, and whatnot, as though they had the official endorsement of Augusta National, which, in truth, wouldn't have endorsed a Second Coming.)

The new winner would don his jacket at The Masters ceremonies by being helped into it by the previous winner, or by Roberts if the winner had repeated. Then Jones would say a few words from his wheelchair to the spectators. Behind him would be rows of officials from all over the world: the president of the USGA, the president of the PGA, the current captain of the Royal and Ancient, and other dignitaries from Spain, Japan, Argentina, and numerous other countries throughout the now vast kingdom of golf in which Jones had once been Arthurian.

Very few in the audience by then had ever seen Bobby Jones swing a golf club, much less win one of his championships. What sat there before them was something close to a ghost. Amateur golf had become almost the exclusive province of college boys, and its national championships were now regarded as little more than kindergartens for the megabuck professional tournament circuit, soon to break away almost altogether from the PGA as the PGA Tour, officially. The Grand Slam was looked upon, even by those few who could tell you what it was, as a tournament trick almost any of the top money-winners could have done at the drop of a Flip-it.

Looking at Bobby Jones in his wheelchair only served to confirm that suspicion. Although his ankles could not be seen, they had become enormously enlarged from body fluids. Conversely, his wrists were as slender as a schoolgirl's. His complexion was Confederate gray, his face jowly, his eyes bloodshot from countless nights without sleep. It would be hard to believe that this was once a man who could effortlessly hit a golf ball an eighth of a mile.

Then Jones would speak. As usual, his thoughts were measured, his words selected, his tone of voice modulated. In his soft drawl, his voice came across to the young as the whispers of grass. But to those who knew who he really was, what he had truly done, and all he had been through, it had the sound of trumpets.

CHAPTER 11:
"CHAMPIONSHIP"

Nobody can say for certain just when The Masters Tournament began to be regarded in the public mind as a major championship. By the early fifties, it was certainly looked upon as the best-run *tournament* in the world. But it wasn't spoken of in the same breath with the Open championships of the United States and Britain or the PGA Championship. They had too much tradition behind them.

In 1950, Jimmy Demaret became the first to win three Masters Tournaments. Since he had yet to win a United States Open or a PGA Championship and never would, and had never so much as entered the British Open, he understandably pronounced The Masters "the greatest championship in the whole world. Bar none!" The press had found in Demaret a refreshing replacement for Walter Hagen, who now played golf not at all. But Demaret's logic didn't come across in print the morning after the night before, as much of Hagen's hadn't. Arguing once that Houston had more to offer as a city than New York, Demaret was asked what Houston had that could top Rockefeller Center. "It's overrated," said Demaret. "Tear it down and what've you got left? A parking lot!"

It would take more than barroom rhetoric to transform The Masters Tournament into a major championship even though it wasn't one and was never meant to be. The year after Demaret's third win, Hogan won his first Masters, then Snead won his second, followed by Hogan, in 1953, winning *his* second. It added to the esteem of The Masters that Hogan in 1953 also won the United States Open, the first time that had happened since before the war. And it added a traditional touch more when Hogan followed up the Open Championship with the British Open. (He would pass up the PGA Championship, then played at match, as he had since 1949, when a ghastly car accident had left emphatic doubts about his life, let alone his golf game. Hogan's battered legs could no longer stand up to successive days of two rounds each. Besides, that year the dates for the PGA conflicted with the British Open's.)

Nobody before had ever won The Masters Tournament, the United States Open, and the British Open in the same year. They formed a new triad, one the public had never so much as thought of.

Proof of sorts came when New York gave Hogan a ticker-tape parade up Broadway when he returned from winning the British Open, which had been at Carnoustie, in Scotland. Would there have been such a parade had Hogan not won The Masters first? Probably not, for the British Open had yet to regain its prewar eminence, not yet being able to offer the sort of prize money that run-of-the-tour events put up almost weekly. It hurt the prestige of The Masters Tournament not at all that Bobby Jones happened to be in New York the day of Hogan's parade. It was only natural for him to be invited to the luncheon in Hogan's honor and then to be seated next to him on the dais. Newspapers had fabricated an argument over who was the better golfer, Jones in his day or Hogan now, and their readers, most of whom had never seen either play, picked up

Ben Hogan, one of the most popular contestants The Masters ever had, lines up his putt. Historic Golf Photos.

the senseless debate among themselves, like teenagers arguing over which is the faster car, a Maserati or a Ferrari. Only two people, it seemed, could see the comparison for the foolishness it was—Bobby Jones and Ben Hogan.

By the time the next Masters Tournament rolled around in April, speculation on the outcome of the event had reached

Sam Snead was the second player ever to win three Masters Tournaments.
Historic Golf Photos.

a new high. Who could stop Hogan? There were a lot of answers in the field, which boasted Snead and Demaret, as usual, plus Mangrum, who had the reputation for not being afraid of anybody, and Byron Nelson, who some people thought could still perform miracles. There was the usual roster of former champions of something or other. But the invitation list, expanded somewhat as the years went by, now included the first twenty-four finishers in past Masters and the United States Open, adding to the roster a whole slew of pros who were on the verge of winning major championships, some of them two or more: Jerry Barber, Jack Burke, Jr., Bob Rosburg, Cary Middlecoff, Tommy Bolt, Chick Harbert, Julius Boros, Jay Hebert, Walter Burkemo, Gene Littler, and, from Australia, Peter Thomson, who that year would win the first of five British Opens, only one less than Harry Vardon's record total.

But the man who did stop Hogan was the least likely of all, an amateur named William Joseph Patton, who was from Morganton, North Carolina, where with such a name you can only be known as "Billy Joe." Patton had qualified by the slimmest of margins, as an alternate on the Walker Cup team. Even here, his selection had been hairline. Patton had never gone beyond the fourth round of the United States Amateur and had failed even to qualify the year before.

Patton made his presence nationally known before the 1954 Masters even officially started. The postwar tournaments had been preceded on Wednesdays by an instructional "clinic" among the pros, which was staged for the spectators on a practice range adjoining the left side of the eighteenth fairway. The show was then followed by a driving contest. Few amateurs had the nerve to enter it, but Billy Joe did. A muscular young man of twenty-eight, he had a home-brewed swing that, next to Snead's or Hogan's, made him look like a drunk at a driving range. Patton won the contest with a drive of 338 yards.

Patton made more news the very next day by tying for the lead with veteran E. J. "Dutch" Harrison. The weather had been cold and blustery, and only two other players had been able to break par—Lloyd Mangrum and Jack Burke, Jr., with 71s. The next day, when the weather turned even worse, Harrison slipped to a 79 and Hogan to a 73, and so Billy Joe, with a 74, took sole possession of the lead at 144. Cary Middlecoff, who was five strokes behind, took a sour glance at the leader board and shook his head at Patton's name at the top. "If this guy wins The Masters," he said, referring to Patton's unorthodox form, "he'll set golf back fifty years."

In the third round, The Masters Tournament began to run true to its past form. (It was the twentieth anniversary of the tournament.) Hogan shot a 69 to Patton's 75, taking a five-stroke lead over him. And Snead had come suddenly to life with a 70, to lead Patton by two. Billy Joe was out of it.

As the leader, Hogan was one of the last to tee off in the final round, followed only by three twosomes who had next to no chance of catching him. As he walked down the third fairway, he heard a thundering roar from the sixth green, which sits out of sight to the left behind a grove of pines. Ordinarily, experienced pros can tell from the volume of a roar of a gallery on another hole just what sort of shot it was for: a shot six feet from the hole, a shot three feet from the hole, a shot that is "stiff." Hogan had not heard a roar quite this loud in a long time. A few seconds later, he saw a familiar face in his gallery, a reporter for a newsmagazine. Hogan gave him a questioning look. The man held up one finger. Patton had just made a hole-in-one.

As Hogan stepped to the sixth tee, he heard a distant roar from the direction of the eighth green. Patton had made a birdie-four.

Just after Hogan drove off the seventh tee, he heard a third roar from near the clubhouse. Patton had birdied the ninth.

They were now even on the card.

But this was Ben Hogan. There were a lot of holes to be played, and he wasn't going to let an amateur he had never heard of dictate how he should play them.

As Hogan stepped to the tenth tee, Patton had just driven off thirteen. Billy Joe's drive had not been as long as some of his others, mainly because he had sliced it, stopping just beyond a conspicuous tree that borders the fairway. From the vicinity of that tree, almost any pro would have laid up short of the water in front of the green, especially under Patton's circumstances. But Billy Joe was an amateur, and he knew such circumstances arise maybe only once in an amateur's lifetime, not every spring. All day he had been bantering with the gallery, which was packed with good ol' boys letting loose with rebel yells and pounding Billy Joe on the back every time they got near him. Billy Joe felt like Davey Crockett with a bear in the sights of his long gun. "Go! Go! Go!" the gallery roared. And so Billy Joe drew a three-wood out of his bag, as if to say, as he later confirmed that he actually had said to himself "Whathehell! I didn't get where I've got by playin' safe!"

The ball sliced to the right again, landing in the water hazard to the right of the green, practically hole-high. The gallery's moan was almost as loud as one of its roars. Studying his lie while Joe Dey, acting as referee, stood by, Patton crawled out of the hazard, sat down, and began to remove his shoes and roll up his pants legs. He was going to try to slap the ball out of the water. The gallery let loose another roar. Patton walked back into the water, had second thoughts about his watery lie, then picked up the ball for a drop behind the hazard that would give him a stroke penalty. Inexplicably, he then played a pitch with his wedge *barefoot*, forgetting to put his shoes back on, or perhaps because he didn't think he needed his spikes. Nobody was sure what Billy Joe might do. The pitch flopped back into the water and Patton ended up with a seven on the hole.

Hogan had driven off the eleventh tee just as Billy Joe had taken his seven on the thirteenth green. That seven had not yet been placed on the leader boards, one of which sits next to the eleventh green. But news of it had spread to Hogan's gallery through the grapevine of spectators that connected clear to Patton's, which was now on the fourteenth tee as Hogan outlined the strategy for his second shot from the eleventh fairway. Probably because of the shell he was famous for withdrawing into during a tournament round, and possibly because all the roars that he heard coming from thirteen were misinterpreted as another birdie by Patton, Hogan was never aware of Patton's double-bogey. Hogan had once said that he didn't mind missing a shot, he just hated missing one before he hit it. That would be the mistake he would make here.

The flagstick on eleven for this round was placed in the lower left-hand corner of the green, nestled between the water in front of the green and a bunker behind it. Ordinarily, Hogan played this hole by giving the entire green a wide berth to the right, content to leave himself a chip or a long putt from off the edge for an almost certain par. He had told other pros that "if you ever see me on this green with my second shot, you'll know I missed it."

Hogan then made one of the very few tactical errors in a career that was noted for their absence. He went directly for the flag-stick. Before the ball had started its descent, veteran observers knew that Hogan had been unaware of Patton's seven. The ball landed in the water on the fly, not twenty feet from the flagstick, but nevertheless in the water.

Hogan dropped for a penalty, and took a six. Patton took a bogey-six on the fifteenth just as Snead finished his round for a total of 289, which Hogan matched by limping home with a 75. The next day in the play-off, Snead won his third Masters Tournament with a 70 to Hogan's 71. Billy Joe, having taken thirteen strokes on two holes, had scored a 71 to finish a stroke behind them.

The beaming smile on Patton's face, though, and the standing ovation he got at the eighteenth green, might have led you to believe he had won. The 1954 Masters Tournament had created a new kind of hero—a give-'em-hell amateur—but nonetheless a hero. You didn't find that type in the major championships any more—the *other* championships.

Patton had come across to the galleries as having something of Bobby Jones about him, a touch of the quality that Jones had said had lifted himself above most of those he played against. Patton *tried* harder. Only, maybe he tried too hard for the sake of the gallery. But his attitude ingratiated him with Augusta National members, notably Jones and Cliff Roberts. Patton was later invited to join the club.

Largely because of Patton, the 1954 Masters Tournament received the nearly weeklong publicity it hadn't received since Jones had competed. Tens of thousands more words were filed through Western Union to newspapers than ever had been from Augusta National's press headquarters, which a few years before had been moved from a tent to a permanent building just beyond the west wing of the expanded clubhouse. All week, Billy Joe Patton had injected into the tournament the fireworks you just couldn't find anymore at championships—other championships—and Snead and Hogan had bolstered the belief that this tournament, when all the shouting was over, was won only by the best there is in golf. The Masters Tournament now had tradition, despite its lack of age. Practically every virtuoso of the steel shaft had now won The Masters Tournament at least once. Now that hickory was dead and long forgotten, no golfer could any longer be considered for greatness unless he did, too.

In 1956, The Masters Tournament was televised for the first time. It had been carried over the radio since its inception by the National Broadcasting Company, but the television contract was awarded to the Columbia Broadcasting System, which was content to produce the show under a number of restrictions by Cliff Roberts, one of which was a time limit on commercials. Augusta National was just as interested in the welfare of spectators who couldn't buy tickets to The Masters Tournament as those who could. Because of those restrictions, the 1956 and 1957 events had no sponsor.

Interested only in a company whose prestige could match Augusta National's, Roberts bided his time until a proper sponsor could be found. That sponsor materialized in 1958 with American Express, which was joined the following year by Travelers Insurance, which remains the oldest continuous sponsor, American Express having dropped out several years later to be replaced, in 1969, by Cadillac. How Cadillac became a sponsor illustrates to what degree of autocracy Cliff Roberts had risen. The story goes that he put a phone call through to Don Ahrens, president of the Cadillac Division of General Motors, and said, "You're it." Ahrens, who had learned to take Roberts's bluntness in stride, was delighted.

Original coverage by television called for a half hour on Fridays and an hour each on Saturdays and Sundays. In 1956, Ken Venturi, an amateur who played like the pro he was about to become, led all the way until Sunday. Then a wind of near gale proportions came up, almost blowing down the camera towers, while Venturi ballooned to an 80. That 80 was not as horrible as it seemed. Only two others in the field that day had been able to break 73: Sam Snead, who had never been in contention, had a 71, as did Jack Burke, Jr., who, as millions watched at home, won by flipping a shot from a bunker by the right-hand side of the last green and then holing a three-footer, all this after hardly having been on camera for two days.

The following year, television had an even sadder fate. Doug Ford holed out of a bunker on the eighteenth hole to win by three strokes—twenty minutes before television went on the air.

In 1958, television might have got a dramatic break. The tournament was won by Arnold Palmer. Unfortunately, though, it was not won in the florid fashion the public would soon come to expect of him. After a rules debacle on the twelfth hole that continued when Palmer reached the thirteenth green, he conferred further with officials before he putted. Then he made the eighteen-footer he had for an eagle-three. But the leader boards and, hence, the television cameras still showed that Palmer had taken a five on the twelfth hole rather than the three he claimed he was entitled to, all this over a temporary embedded-ball rule deemed "local" because of an all-night rain.

More discussion between Palmer and officials followed on the fourteenth hole. The argument was finally settled on the fifteenth hole in his favor, giving Palmer a three on the twelfth rather than the five the public thought he had. Everybody was confused as well as surprised that he was now leading by two strokes. But then, in something less than the style that would become expected of him, he took two bogeys on the last three holes. Palmer won his first Masters Tournament sitting in the clubhouse while first Doug Ford and then pro Fred Hawkins tried vainly to catch him. Strapped with only sixty minutes of air time, and a situation so befuddling that even officials weren't sure what was going on, television had nothing dramatic to capture. Viewers had to read Monday morning's papers to find out how Arnold Palmer, whose name a lot of them were unfamiliar with, had actually won The Masters.

The very next year, television was put into another tournament situation its early production facilities couldn't keep up with. Two years before, a cut in the field of The Masters had been instituted after the first two rounds for the low forty players and ties. Art Wall had made it in 1959 with only two strokes to spare. But now, with only a 71 in the third round and six strokes behind, he was playing well ahead of the leaders in the final round. Then, in the kind of finish that hadn't been seen since Byron Nelson at his best, Wall birdied five of the last six holes while the cameras were concentrating on Palmer and Canadian Stan Leonard, who had been leading, and on Dick Mayer, who was trying to catch them, along with Cary Middlecoff, who very well might. Middlecoff had won two United States Opens and, back in 1955, this very Masters Tournament. But they didn't catch Art Wall and he won by a stroke. Television announcers sat on the towers holding their heads in their hands.

Television finally got a break in the 1960 Masters. Starting off with a 67, Arnold Palmer led the field every day and clear through the last round until the "par-four-and-a-half" fifteenth, which he was expected to birdie and hadn't, just as he also hadn't the equally birdieable thirteenth. Ken Venturi, now a pro and playing ahead of Palmer, posted a 70 for 283, and then sat down in the clubhouse to watch Palmer on a television monitor. Palmer would have to make a birdie on either seventeen or eighteen to tie him. Either possibility was unlikely, so Venturi relaxed.

Palmer lined up a twenty-seven-foot putt on the seventeenth green, then twice walked away from it uncertainly, as though he felt there was no possible way of getting this putt close to the hole. Finally he rapped the ball. It was an unusually cautious putt for him. It looked short all the way. It crept toward the hole, hung on the lip a fraction of a second, and then dropped in.

Venturi sat up in his chair.

On the eighteenth, Palmer, punching a six-iron for his second shot, almost hit the flag-stick on the fly. The ball spun back five feet below the cup.

Venturi was on the edge of his seat.

Palmer studied the putt quickly, like a fighter who has his man on the ropes. Then he stepped into it, flashed it into the hole, and won the tournament outright.

Venturi stood up. "Was that *real?*" he asked nobody in particular, as though what he had seen might have been a dramatized commercial. "I thought I was looking at a Vitalis ad!"

Palmer had a pugnacious manner about him on the golf course that appealed to those spectators more oriented toward contact sports. He had a way of walking to a tee unlike other pros, most of whom did so as though they were waiting for a bus to come along. Palmer didn't so much walk onto a tee as he did climb into it, as though it were a prize ring, and then he would look around at the gallery as though he were searching for somebody brave enough to fight him.

The shots Palmer hit weren't hit at all. They were over-powered. Even a pitch with his wedge had a way of pulling his shirttail out, and he was forever tucking it in and then hitching up his trousers, which was not for show. While Palmer had the arms and shoulders of a piano-mover, he had the waistline of a chorus boy.

Where some pros could project to the galleries with their facial expressions, Palmer used his whole body. Missing a six-foot

Arnold Palmer's exciting body language helped recruit his immense army of fans. Historic Golf Photos.

putt, he might drop to his knees, as though the world had come to an end. Holing a six-footer, he might jump a yard in the air, throw his ball the length of an eight-iron to the crowd, and bear-hug his caddie. You could walk an entire round without seeing one ball Palmer hit and still know where his shots had gone. All you had to do was read his body English.

From the 1960 Masters Tournament on, Arnold Palmer would be known everywhere as "Arnie," although few people had called him that before the tournament. At that Masters, he picked up a whole battalion of fans who thought he could do no wrong. Two months later, he would have his own army.

Arnie's Army was not recruited overnight, as has since been myopically recounted. The rebel yells that had once been spent on Billy Joe Patton were aimed at Palmer during that Masters Tournament, and the crews at several leader boards had posted the message, "Go, Arnie, Go!" (Cliff Roberts soon put a stop to that.) But it would take television to put together an entire army.

That year—1960—an invention was introduced to television that the public soon took for granted but which would revolutionize the industry as surely as the long-playing record had the phonograph, leading as that invention had to high fidelity recording techniques and eventually stereophonic sound. Television's innovation was videotape. With it, television could have recapped most of Jack Burke's final round back in 1956, Doug Ford's bunker shot at eighteen in '57, the three Palmer scored on the twelfth instead of the five the leader boards had reported in '58, and all five of Art Wall's birdies during the last six holes. In 1960, it didn't need this new invention when Palmer brought the climax to the very last green. But it would in the future. Arnie's Army wanted to know where its general was all the time, winning or losing, even if he were already in the clubhouse.

Videotape was also not needed at the United States Open that Palmer won only weeks after that second Masters Tournament. That championship was carried live, and due to the two-hour difference in time from Cherry Hills, in Denver, it was shown in the populous East during prime time. It was *then* that Arnie's Army was formed. But it would do most of its marching at Augusta National, where for the next four years The Masters Tournament became its favorite battlefield and where television could show the public almost every shot fired.

It was only natural that, after Cherry Hills, Palmer would play in the British Open, which in 1960 was its centennial—although, due to two world wars, only eighty-eight championships actually had been played—and which therefore was fittingly played over the Old Course at St. Andrews.

Palmer did not win it, although he would the following two years in a row. But before Palmer even teed off at St. Andrews, the public was thinking that if he did win it, and then the PGA Championship later on that year, he would have won what they were beginning to call the "Big Four." The Masters Tournament was now a major championship, in fact if not in name. As the years went by, everybody—even Masters officials—referred without hesitation to the tournament as a championship, and the winner of it as its champion.

One afternoon Bobby Jones was watching play with a friend on a monitor that had been set up in his cottage. Nobody else was present. Jones heard a television announcer refer to The Masters as a "championship" one more time than he could bear without comment. "Championship of *what?*" he asked. He did not expect an answer. He just disliked the term, as he had disliked calling the Augusta National Invitation the "Masters Tournament." But he knew now, as then, that he was shouting down the wind.

CHAPTER 12:
IN PERPETUITY

As Byron Nelson had his Sam Snead and then both Snead and Ben Hogan to contend with, so would Arnold Palmer have his Gary Player and then both Player and Jack Nicklaus. It seems to have been always thus in golf. You could look clear back to Harry Vardon and sensibly question if he would have won those record six British Opens had not J. H. Taylor and then James Braid both won five, thereby pushing Vardon's career to heights he might otherwise not have reached.

From Johannesburg, South Africa, Player came to his first Masters Tournament in 1956 under a special exemption that had been instituted a few years before to make the tournament even closer to universal than it already was. Invitations were extended to outstanding players from foreign countries—Japan, Spain, Italy—who had not won the British Open or Amateur or could not be on Ryder or Walker Cup teams. Player was then only twenty, but had already been a professional for three years. That year, he had won the South African Open for the first of what would be thirteen times. Three years later, he won the British Open and, in 1961, The Masters by nosing out Palmer and amateur Charlie Coe by a stroke.

Coe was a slender, plodding sort of golfer who had won two United States Amateurs. (He would later become a member at Augusta National.) But unlike Billy Joe Patton's situation back in 1954, hardly anybody knew that Coe was in contention for The Masters in 1961, in part because he came out of nowhere with 69s for his last two rounds and in larger part because all eyes were on Palmer, who needed only a par on the final hole to win outright, a bogey-five to tie Player.

Trapped in the bunker to the right of the eighteenth green in two, Palmer "skulled" the ball over the green, pitched back eight feet past the cup, and then missed the putt, ending up with a double-bogey-six. "That," he said, referring to his fumbling finish, "is something I thought only happened to other people."

When Player won the PGA Championship the following year, he had won three of the Big Four, all except the United States Open, which he would win in 1965 but never again. Still, you couldn't help but think he might just possibly win three, if not all, of the Big Four in one year when he won The Masters again in 1974 and 1978, particularly since he had won the PGA Championship again in 1972 and two more British Opens in 1968 and 1974. Player's problem—if you wanted to call it a problem—was that only in 1974 could he pack two titles back to back into the same season. But neither included The Masters Tournament, which, heading the championship calendar as it does, was now the springboard event for the Big Four.

Palmer again won The Masters in 1962, after a play-off with his pal Dow Finsterwald and with Player, defending. And Palmer would win it for his fourth and final time two years later, becoming the first to do so. By this time, he had also become the most electric gallery attraction in the game since Bobby Jones and, on television, an electronic folk hero. He would remain so clear into his fifties, and not just on the senior tour that had been economically possible largely because tournament sponsors knew Arnie's Army would follow him anywhere. On the PGA Tour itself, he still commanded larger galleries than any other pro until he faded hopelessly out of contention.

People who knew no more about golf than what they could see on television while sitting in a Barcalounger at home or having a beer at a neighborhood bar had no trouble at all understanding what Palmer was doing on a golf course. They could tell from the by-now familiar expressions on his famous face and the by-now ceremonial contortions of his pugilistic body. The other pros—well, on a nineteen-inch screen they came across as so many faces in the crowd, nameless nonentities who all looked alike and dressed the same, strangers in a tournament paradise where you could earn a small fortune without winning a single tournament.

But Arnie Palmer was something else again. He was Sid Caesar, Frank Gifford, and Mr. Clean all wrapped into one. The fact that he was playing golf was incidental. He had the physical magnetism that makes for superstardom; ordinary viewers dropped what they were doing when he came on screen. Palmer would thus forever be "the champ," the way prizefighters on the order of Jack Dempsey were hailed years after their heydays were over.

By a kind of inverse logic, Palmer thereby elevated The Masters Tournament further in the public's estimation as a major national championship. He had won two British Opens; indeed, had almost single-handedly restored that championship to its historical importance internationally. But he never would win another United States Open after that one in 1960, and would not win a PGA Championship at all. But he *had* won The Masters Tournament, and four times at that. The Masters therefore could be thought of as nothing other than a championship, perhaps the most important of all. If you didn't believe so, all you had to do was ask the man in the Barcalounger, the guy in the neighborhood bar, the housewife with a broom in her hand. They knew who "the champ" was, even though by now whoever actually was the champion might be one of those what's-his-names.

If Palmer, with those four Masters Tournaments under his belt, had become a Siegfried in the epic of golf, by 1965 the public was therefore at a loss to categorize Jack Nicklaus. So, through no fault of his own, Nicklaus became golf's anti-hero, mainly because he was beginning to dethrone Palmer at the game of which nongolfers and even some first-generation golfers thought Palmer was the once and future king. But older, more experienced tournament observers knew Nicklaus would be somebody to behold.

There was an inkling that Nicklaus was on his way to playing supragolf—golf not seen since Bobby Jones at his grandest—when he won the 1959 United States Amateur at the age of nineteen, defeating in the final the vastly more experienced Charlie Coe. The following year, still an amateur and paired with Ben Hogan for the last two rounds, he might have won the United States Open at Cherry Hills that Palmer won. (And he would have, as Hogan would say afterward sympathetically, "by five shots if I could have done his thinking for him.") Then, in 1961, he won a second United States Amateur before turning professional.

As a pro, Nicklaus did not help his public image any by weighing a shade over a chunky two hundred pounds, about twenty more than his five-foot-eleven frame called for, prompting the unkindly nickname in the press, "Fat Jack." He

An anti-hero to some, Jack Nicklaus would eventually win a record of five Masters Tournaments. Historic Golf Photos.

unwittingly emphasized that weight by wearing the sort of skintight clothes that might have made him big-man-on-campus at Ohio State but which at big-time golf tournaments made him look as though he were there to collect autographs. Between shots, he could walk your legs off, so brisk was his pace. But his actual playing was maddeningly deliberate.

There were a number of valid reasons for this slowness. To begin with, Nicklaus did not know the courses that he would be playing during that first swing around the tournament circuit in 1962. So he paced off all his drives in practice rounds, subtracted the distance from the scorecard, and then, after spotting a sprinkler head or some other reference point, kept meticulous notes of how far he was from the greens—the front, center, and rear of them. Then, in the tournament itself he played each shot with a premeditation that spectators, and television viewers in particular, found exasperating.

But Nicklaus knew precisely what he was doing. He might have been young, but he understood that he had a long, long career ahead of him, during which he was going to drain every ounce of championship golf that he could from a native talent that saw him breaking par at twelve and breaking course records before he was out of high school. And that talent became obvious almost as soon as he turned professional in 1962, so much so that soon every pro on the tour began pacing off courses and keeping notebooks. In time, even duffers started pacing off their home courses, although some of them shot scores that looked like area codes. Jack does it, the thinking went, so why shouldn't I?

Almost immediately upon turning professional, Nicklaus started collecting national golf titles with the effortless regularity of an Eagle Scout collecting merit badges. In 1962, when he was twenty-two, he won the United States Open, no less, by winning a play-off at treacherous Oakmont, fittingly enough, against Arnie Palmer, God forbid! The following year he won The Masters in wet, windy weather that left the course so saturated that play was almost called off on two different days. Augusta National had never played longer. In all four days, only one other man was able to break 69—Gene Littler with a 68 on the last day when he was way out of the picture. Nicklaus shot a 66 in the second round and, after that, nobody could catch him.

By 1966, Nicklaus had won a PGA Championship and would win his third Masters, this in a play-off against Tommy Jacobs and Gay Brewer that took more than five hours, ending close to darkness. Veteran sportswriter Jimmy Burns of the *Miami Herald* grew weary of creeping around the course after four hours and went into the clubhouse to watch the finish on a television monitor. As the three pros trudged to the eighteenth green in the twilight, Burns shook his head philosophically. "This," he said to nobody in particular, "is what killed horseshoes."

By the time he had reached twenty-eight, the age at which Bobby Jones had retired, Nicklaus had won nine "majors," only four less than Jones's collection of national championships. The inevitable comparisons between the two began, just as they had fifteen years before between Jones and Ben Hogan. Nicklaus's followers pointed out that Jack had not been eligible for amateur championships since six years before, ignoring the fact that Jones had never been eligible for the PGA Championship and had been the inspiration for The Masters Tournament, a "title" that by then constituted three of the "championships" Jack had won.

On and on the inanities went. At last, Jones could remain silent no longer. He stifled the argument for good with a touch of the royal rhetoric that had so marked both his personal and public life. "Jack Nicklaus," he said graciously, "plays a game with which I am not familiar."

And it was. Indeed, it was a game with which nobody was familiar. To begin with, Nicklaus was then the longest, straightest driver in the history of championship golf. While one or two other pros could hit the ball as far in tournaments now and again, none seemed able to maintain that length and still hit the fairways during championships. Often overlooked was how outrageously long Nicklaus was with his irons, and it stands to reason that he could be more accurate with his seven-iron where other pros were forced to use five-irons.

Some people, none of whom had ever watched Jones during his prime, said Nicklaus was the greatest putter the game had known. (Few of them had ever seen Bobby Locke in action, either—not to mention Walter Hagen.) But Nicklaus was undeniably a truly great putter, particularly at the birdie range between eight and twenty feet. Certainly, he never hit a careless putt in his life. The only time he would one-hand a putt was when it was hanging on the lip, sometimes not even then, and never in exasperation. Even in his forties, as his game naturally began to decline, he would line up a putt on the last green of a tournament to finish maybe twenty-fifth. That putt might be only two feet long, but Jack would study and stroke it as though his entire career depended on it. If Nicklaus had a recognizable weakness, it might be said to have been his play out of bunkers. But, then, you had to take note of how few bunkers he had ever been in.

What really distinguished Nicklaus from Jones and Jones's contemporaries in the age of hickory was the way Jack *attacked* a golf course, as Palmer and then Player did, and as eventually every pro who wanted to play like them would have to. Jones seldom if ever tried to outmuscle a golf course, most noticeably off the tee, when he only went all out with his driver if he thought the odds were distinctly in his favor. Nicklaus & Company went all out off every tee, even if it meant driving with an iron. Jones, by contrast, played with what J. H. Taylor had called "courageous timidity." To put the situation another way, Jones made the golf course come to *him*. Then he would counterpunch it into submission.

Even on the greens there was a different philosophy, although Jones may have been the greatest pressure putter the game has seen. Nicklaus putted as though every putt was holeable, even from sixty feet. (Palmer thought every *chip* was holeable.) But Nicklaus might not have if he had been faced with the greens Jones had to putt over, before greenkeepers had the agronomic advantages of fungicides, insecticides, and other chemicals that are taken for granted today. So Jones putted with that dying ball, when three-putting was a constant reality, and it seems incredible that he holed as many long putts as he did. (A putt he once holed at St. Andrews was later measured off at forty *yards*.) But the dying ball was a caution Nicklaus and his camp could no longer afford, not with the winner's share of prize money running into six figures and when a smart agent could convert a string of "majors" into endorsements that would lead to an income running into seven figures. If you didn't hole those forty-footers, there were too many other pros out there who would.

Whatever his strengths or weaknesses, Nicklaus did himself proud by going on record as saying that, although he had never seen him play, the golfer he had admired most in life was Bobby Jones. And there was not one note of pity in his words.

Eventually, Nicklaus would add up a total of nineteen of the "majors": two United States Amateurs, three British

Opens, four United States Opens, five PGA Championships, and five Masters Tournaments. Three of those subtotals were records, although two of them were only historical ties. His total of four United States Opens was a record that had been established, back in what Nicklaus-followers considered golf's Ice Age, by an all-but-forgotten pro named Willie Anderson, five years after the turn of the century. It was tied by Jones in 1930 and by Hogan in 1953. And Nicklaus's five PGA Championships matched a record set by Walter Hagen back in 1927. Considering the depth of Nicklaus's competition, all in all it was an awesome total.

But of that total, only those five Masters Tournaments was a record distinctively Nicklaus's own. It was the record that most impressed the public while he was in the process of setting it, packed as those five were within thirteen years, three of them within four years. Whatever else he might have done in golf—and that record of nineteen "majors" might well stand forever—Jack Nicklaus had established once and for all that The Masters is The Masters is The Masters. There was no other tournament or championship quite like it. It was the tournament most golfers would most like to win. And, in 1985, poll taken by a golf publication among PGA Tour members, American and foreign, affirmed that as an overwhelming fact.

As Nicklaus drew abreast of Palmer and Player on the championship ledger, there was talk in golf circles of the Big Four becoming a "professional Grand Slam," as though there were some historical parallel between what a pro could do in the future and what Bobby Jones had done as an amateur back in 1930—which there wasn't. The odds against winning the Big Four in a single season were stratospheric.

In chronological order, they were The Masters Tournament, the United States Open, the British Open, and finally the

PGA Championship. To be sure, Palmer had won the first two back in 1960. But twelve years afterward, only Nicklaus was able to put the first two back to back again, much less the first three, let alone all four. Talk of a professional Grand Slam dropped out of even locker-room conversation.

Then, in 1985, a kid amateur still in college, named Scott Verplank, won the Western Open against a whole field of PGA Tour pros. Golfers who understood something about the different natures of both stroke- and match-play began to hypothesize. With his amateur standing somehow restored to him, could a *professional* win the Grand Slam that Jones had miraculously put together fifty-five years before? That is, could he win both the United States Open and the British Open? And, in the process, could he win thirteen straight matches in the United States Amateur and the British Amateur? There were a lot of young amateurs out there, as young Verplank had shown, who weren't afraid of anybody, amateur *or* pro. Johnny Goodman had proved that in the first round at Pebble Beach back in 1929 against the Emperor Jones himself.

It was an interesting hypothesis, albeit a false one historically. But it evoked the dimensions of the original Grand Slam. Had there been a fourth dimension back then that Bobby Jones had gone into? Something in time-space?

As The Masters Tournament became the all-but-exclusive province of Demaret, Snead, and Hogan, and then of Palmer, Player, and Nicklaus, it altogether naturally grew more famous in the press and richer in prize money than it had been in those off-years when it was won by pros of less renown. Concomitantly—and altogether naturally—it grew in Cliff Roberts's mind, preoccupied as he had been all his adult life with both the rich and the famous. Whereas, before the Second World War, Roberts's position as tournament chairman had been an avocation, it became after the war a passion and, in time, an *idée-force*. The job colored his behavior, and that behavior pulled The Masters out of the ranks of ordinary tournaments and pushed it into the forefront of championships, even though it wasn't one.

In 1948, Roberts served notice to contestants that they would only be allowed to play one ball in practice rounds. A regular on the tournament circuit then (in a category that no longer exists) was Frank Stranahan, who was good enough to play against the pros and wealthy enough to do so as an amateur. In point of fact, he had tied for second with Byron Nelson in The Masters just the year before, a stroke ahead of Hogan but two behind Demaret. Stranahan enjoyed the company of professionals and considered himself one of them, as they did him, despite his amateur status.

At that 1948 Masters, Stranahan misinterpreted Roberts's ruling, thinking it applied only to three or four contestants playing together, and certainly not to somebody playing by himself. Stranahan was mistaken. Playing alone, and thereby holding up the play of nobody else, he played a second ball to several greens. On the back nine, he was requested to leave the course and told that his invitation had been withdrawn. Stranahan was nonplussed.

But Roberts was adamant. When a few members reminded Roberts that Bob Stranahan, Frank's father and chairman of the board of Champion Spark Plugs, was a highly respected figure in golf throughout the world, Roberts stared them down. Stranahan was out of the tournament, and that was that. Frank packed his bags and went on to the next event.

But the word had gone out, as Roberts undoubtedly knew it would. The pros now understood that if Roberts would throw Frank Stranahan out of The Masters, he wouldn't brook any nonsense from them, either. Nor would they have any appeal through the PGA. This was The Masters Tournament, by invitation only, not the Lower Rio Grande Valley Fruit and Vegetable Open in Harlingen, Texas, where they had played just the month before.

At that time, amateurs were distinguished from professionals on scoreboards everywhere with an asterisk in front of their names, a practice that had replaced the old, elitist custom of distinguishing them by printing "Mr." in front. Bobby Jones had always had an asterisk in front of his name during The Masters, patently because everybody knew he wouldn't accept prize money.

Just the year before the Stranahan incident, a former Boston newspaperman named Bob Harlow had launched *Golf World*, a weekly newsmagazine devoted to golf that was financed in part by Frank's father, Bob Stranahan. While Harlow was an eloquent admirer of Jones, he had made his name in golf circles as, first, Walter Hagen's manager and, later, as an early and almost forgotten manager of the PGA's tournament bureau. When Frank Stranahan was ordered off the course at Augusta National, Harlow was understandably peeved. Cornering Roberts, he asked, apropos of nothing, how Bob Jones could have an asterisk before his name when he was a professional in fact if not in practice?

Here, indeed, was a sore point. For the first time since his retirement in 1930, Jones's state of limbo between amateurism and professionalism was being questioned. What with *Golf World* now in back of Harlow (not to mention Bob Stranahan), perhaps it might end up being questioned publicly. (The R & A had thought it had solved the problem by declaring Jones an amateur "for life," regardless of how much money he made off the game while not playing. But that distinction wouldn't hold water with the USGA nor, for that matter, with Jones himself. Frankly, Jones didn't care what people thought he was.)

If Harlow or anybody else believed he could place Cliff Roberts between the horns of a dilemma, he was sadly underestimating the acumen of Augusta National's chairman. Roberts heard Harlow out. He studied the main scoreboard for a few minutes, grunted in his habitual manner, and then walked off.

The following morning the asterisks in front of every amateur's name had been removed. They have stayed so ever since. If you didn't know an amateur from a pro—the implication clearly became—then you had no license watching a Masters Tournament.

Until 1960, you had to keep track of the leaders at The Masters just as you did at every other golf tournament: by looking at the hole-by-hole scores on a scoreboard and then quickly calculating against par who was leading. If seven or eight players were in contention, this could lead to arithmetic that some spectator's were not quick at. Even players themselves sometimes got confused. The system was so time-honored, though, that nobody gave a thought to improving it. But Cliff Roberts did.

Putting his head together with some members', Roberts devised a unique "over-and-under" method of posting scores. On the scoreboards, which are in sight all over Augusta National, the scores were calculated for you in respect to each leading player's standing with par. Red numerals indicated how many under par he stood, green numerals how many over par. Even-par scores were indicated by a green zero. You could now tell at a glance how everybody who had a chance of leading stood at any given moment. In short, Roberts had now fixed things so that you didn't even have to think at The Masters.

So many tournament innovations had started at The Masters that it had become a game in itself among long-time spectators wondering what Roberts would come up with next. Even long-time contestants sometimes had to shake their heads in amusement. Still, if you weren't sharp, some of those innovations might go unnoticed. But they were there—every year.

One year, a few pros who thought they had seen everything at golf tournaments found a novelty that left some of them baffled at first. Small signs about a foot square had been stuck in the ground just in front of the practice range. The signs informed the players at what height, to within an eighth of an inch, the turf on the range had been mowed. The signs noted that this height was the same as the turf on the fairways.

What was the purpose? You might want to keep track of how high and far your ball would bounce and roll before you got out on the course.

In 1966, two bunkers were constructed to the left of the landing area of the eighteenth fairway, thereby narrowing its width to thirty yards. The idea was strictly Roberts's own, with Jones's reluctant approval, although for some curious reason Roberts did not want to take credit.

Contestants who did not play in their first Masters until after the bunkers had been constructed complained to each other that they were not fair, this in a game that was never meant to be fair, only equitable. The bunkers were precisely where they wanted to hit a straight drive. Now they were forced to fade their tee shots away from the bunkers and dangerously close to the trees on the right.

Fair or not, everybody who had been going to The Masters before 1966 knew why they were there. They were supposed to stop Jack Nicklaus, who from the very start of his first Masters had been bombing his drives to that part of the fairway, from which they bounded into the practice range that borders it, leaving him with only a wedge shot or, at most, a nine-iron to the green. With his gargantuan length, he was making a mockery of the hole.

Even more curious than Roberts not wanting to take credit for the bunkers was his persistence in referring to the two bunkers in the singular. "The bunker," he called them. During the annual interview Roberts gave in the tournament room just before each Masters began, a young reporter asked the year they were put in if Roberts didn't mean two bunkers. No, Roberts said. There's only one bunker on the eighteenth fairway. The reporter began to scratch his head. Veteran golf writers smiled at one another. If Cliff Roberts said one plus one only adds up to one, that's it. There were no two ways about it. (Several years later, Roberts began to hedge. He referred to the bunkers as a "two-section bunker"—whatever that is.)

As Roberts became more and more obsessed with the Masters Tournament after the war, he was several times referred to in print as a "curmudgeon," a word, largely overused in political columns, that had once been a synonym for "avaricious" but had then become a polite word for somebody who thought that the only right way to do things was his way. In that sense, the appellation was correct. Roberts did insist on doing things his way. But he didn't arrive at his way without a great deal of consultation and forethought. Cliff Roberts's decisions were not always popular decisions, particularly since he never stooped to rationalize them. But they were never hasty decisions.

For all his foibles, his peccadillos, his sometimes infuriating idiosyncrasies—chiefly, an almost total inability to tell you in plain words what he was thinking—Roberts made himself into the one indispensable figure at Augusta National and at The Masters Tournament. This was true of him more so than even

Bobby Jones, who was too tender-hearted and, later, too crippled to be a take-charge tournament chairman. Cliff Roberts was, in the last analysis, an autocrat in the absolute, and that is what all golf clubs and all golf tournaments need above anything else if they are going to venture into the extraordinary.

Assuredly, nobody else at Augusta National coveted his job, and there were a lot of executives at the club who could take power in stride. And that job had cost Roberts large amounts of time and energy that could have been spent at his New York office putting together what inarguably would have been a financial estate much larger than it actually was. But he never had any regrets about what his achingly long work at Augusta National had cost him in business opportunities. Comparing what he might have made on Wall Street to what he got out of Augusta National, he waxed sentimental. "Briefly stated," he wrote near the end of his days, "I've been overpaid."

In the mid-seventies, Roberts discovered that he was terminally ill, and his health declined alarmingly after the 1977 Masters Tournament. On September 29, he died, as his mother had, a suicide, leaving a note of apology to his wife attached to the hopeless medical prognosis his physicians had given him not long before. It's been rumored that he is buried on the golf course, having sworn club officials to secrecy exactly where. If true, it is altogether fitting that his grave remain a secret. In life, he was a very private person. Surely he should be allowed to remain so in death.

Roberts was given the title of "Chairman in Memoriam" after he died. For several years, though, he had been training a Houston businessman named William H. Lane to succeed him, and everybody wondered how the mild-mannered Lane could possibly step into Roberts's shoes. They had scant chance to find out. Lane served only two years as chairman before he too became desperately ill. Just before the 1979 Masters Tournament, he suffered a cranial aneurysm, from which he never recovered. He died the following year while still in his fifties and, officially, while still in office.

Soon after Bill Lane took office, it became obvious that Cliff Roberts's job was too big for any normal executive, particularly since the tournament was growing bigger and more complex by the year. So the club elected a vice-chairman. The choice was Hord W. Hardin, then sixty-six, a lawyer and banker from St. Louis who was in semiretirement. The vote had been unanimous.

On record, Hardin was superbly qualified to take over as chairman after Bill Lane died, perhaps more so than even Cliff Roberts had been. Hardin had worked his way up the executive ladder of the USGA until, in 1968, he was elected its president. (Roberts had never been elected an officer of anything.) So Hardin, like Roberts, knew how major championships are supposed to be run. He was a recognized expert on the multifarious rules of the game, which Roberts had never been, and those rules had a variety of ways of being misinterpreted almost daily during The Masters. And through the USGA, Hardin, like Roberts, had come to be known by everybody who was anybody in high-echelon golf.

On top of all these qualifications, Hardin in his younger days had been an excellent amateur golfer, way beyond any golf that Roberts may even have dreamed of playing. Hardin had four times qualified for the United States Amateur and, in 1952, for the United States Open. All that didn't make him a tour pro, but it helped when it came time to look one in the eye.

A big, strapping man, Hardin held an image of authority. In front of an audience, such as press interviews, he came across as refreshingly nonabrasive after Cliff Roberts, and some sportswriters thought for this reason he might lose the reins on a tournament that had a tendency to rear up. But when they were alone with him, writers were surprised at how two-fisted Hardin's thinking could be.

The important thing was that Augusta National members held Hardin in respect, as did the far-flung committee members who showed up every April to help run The Masters Tournament. None of them envied Hardin his job. Indeed, what may have kept them all content was the fear that Hardin might suddenly ask one of them if he would like to take over the keys to the Augusta National kingdom.

Hord Hardin wasn't any Cliff Roberts. But then, everybody had to ask himself, who else was? Whatever *he* was, Hardin continued to chair both Augusta National and The Masters Tournament to the satisfaction of everyone who had the vaguest conception of how thankless the near-endless task was. What few critics he had in his initial years probably couldn't have run a lemonade stand, and even they soon disappeared. Jones unquestionably would have approved of Hardin as Roberts's successor.

Bobby Jones had died in the early evening of December 18, 1971, at his home in Atlanta while asleep. As his doctors had predicted, it was not syringomyelia that killed him. It was an aneurysm. Even that took days and days longer than expected.

His burial was in Atlanta's Oakland Cemetery with only the immediate family in attendance. His tombstone reads:

ROBERT TYRE JONES, JR.
BORN 1902   DIED 1971

No other words were thought necessary. Certainly, Jones wouldn't have added any.

Jones on the sidelines, having last played in 1948. Historic Golf Photos.

Augusta National named him "President in Perpetuity."

Obituaries throughout the world were glowing, some of them having been prepared by writers whom Jones outlived. The public, almost none of whom had ever seen him play, gathered from the obituaries that he had once been a young, rich amateur who won a lot of big tournaments, some of them against professionals, because he didn't do anything but play golf. Then he quit, most readers presumed, because he had sense enough not to try to play against the big boys.

What the obituaries didn't say was this: Some men who played golf after Jones had hit the ball farther, some maybe straighter. Certainly, many had scored lower. A lot of them had won way more tournaments and one of them, Jack Nicklaus, more championships. But nobody had ever played golf *like* Bobby Jones.

And nobody ever would.

Jones had not been able to go to a Masters Tournament for three years, and had not ventured outside his cottage by the tenth tee for two years before that. There he had held court for groups of old pros, golf writers, visiting firemen, foreign golf dignitaries, Atlanta and Augusta friends of long standing, and those Augusta National members who would talk shop and lay off the good ol' days. Jones had no stomach for sentimentalism, abhorred talk for talk's sake, and was too proud for pity.

The question of Jones's status as an amateur or professional, ghoulishly enough, still had a way of coming up nearly twenty years after he had last had a club in his hands and nearly ten years after he had been able to walk. In 1962, the USGA decided they would go along with the R & A's policy of declaring Jones an amateur for life, just for nostalgia's sake. As a matter of not altogether serious formality, the USGA sent him its standard form for reinstatement as an amateur.

Present occupation? the form asked. Jones wrote, "Assistant."

Employer? Jones wrote, "Clifford Roberts."

Do you understand the Rules of Amateur Status? Jones wrote, "Hell, no."

Without any mental reservations, have you decided permanently to abandon all activities contrary to those Rules? Jones wrote, "I have no mental reservations about anything."

What difference did it make whether you were an amateur or a pro when you could quit the golf scene with that kind of dignified humor? Jones left the argument to be settled by those who claimed that he never beat anybody who was any good, that the courses he played over were easier, that the scores he made weren't low enough to compare to today's. In short, to those who tried to defame him when Ben Hogan and then Jack Nicklaus came along.

In 1958, Jones was made a freeman of the Royal Burgh of St. Andrews, Scotland. Before the ceremony, which was staged in a hall that held two thousand people and needed to accommodate two thousand more, Jones had no idea of what the honor meant. All he knew was that the Old Course there was his favorite in all the world and that the citizens had a warmth he had never known elsewhere. He dismissed the ceremony as something on the order of getting a key to a city in America, which he considered "largely an excuse to have the visitor's, and incidentally the mayor's, picture printed in the afternoon newspaper.

St. Andrews is far more than a golf resort. John Knox once preached from one of its churches. Mary Queen of Scots was held political prisoner in one of its castles. And St. Andrews University, one of the most respected in the English-speaking world, was founded in 1413. No more than a dozen persons, from poets to politicians, had ever been granted the honor that Jones was about to receive. The last American to have been so honored was Benjamin Franklin.

Jones had been requested to prepare a speech. He did not. He never considered himself a good speechmaker. He preferred to speak extemporaneously, elaborating on whatever words he had been introduced by. And so he had never been able to write out a speech beforehand. But when he got to the hall, he began to think perhaps he should have.

The pomp was overwhelming, and the ceremony very formal. The stage was banked with flowers, mainly roses, which in Scotland can grow to the size of cabbages. The provost, or mayor, and other dignitaries of St. Andrews were gowned in crimson robes with wide ermine collars. The provost, whom Jones had met only a few days before, gave an eloquent tribute to Jones, recounting his golf career in detail and ending on a touching note about the special affection St. Andreans held for "our Bobby."

As Jones pushed himself to his feet on his leg braces to reply, he recalled years later, "I found out how a man's life, or a great part of it, can flash through his mind in an instant." In that instant, a very minor episode at the Old Course from twenty-two years before came back to him. He had considered that episode the most touching of his career.

The year was 1936. Jones and his wife had sailed with Grantland Rice and his wife to Southampton en route to the Olympic Games in Berlin. On board the ship, the party ran into Bob Woodruff, of the Coca-Cola Company, and Woodruff's wife, who were with a party of friends also on their way to the Games. But, first, they had planned to go to Gleneagles, the inland golf resort only a short drive from St. Andrews. Jones and his party were persuaded to join them. On the offhand chance he might want to play somewhere while abroad, Jones had brought his clubs with him.

At Gleneagles, Jones could not resist being that close to the Old Course without playing it once again. He had not been back since the British Amateur of the Grand Slam six years before. Everybody decided to drive to St. Andrews the next morning and play the Old Course that afternoon.

When Jones got to the first tee, he was astounded to see a gallery of several thousand waiting for him, the word that he was coming having leaked out. Rice, Woodruff, and the others stepped aside, letting Jones play the round for the benefit of the gallery while Willie Auchterlonie, the Royal and Ancient's honorary professional, stepped in as playing companion.

Jones had not been playing much golf, and what little he was playing had been horrible. But on this day the atmosphere at St. Andrews inspired him. The gallery was *with* him, not just for him. As soon as he effortlessly parred the first hole, he knew the old "feel" had returned. His clubs felt like obedient extensions of his mind. For one more shining hour, at least, he knew he was going to be able to perform the way he once had in national championships

Jones made a birdie-three at the second, a birdie-four at the fifth, played a run-up in true St. Andrews fashion through the swale in front of the sixth green for another birdie-three, and parred the seventh with a four.

By this time, the word that "Bobby's back" had spread all over St. Andrews, and Jones's gallery had grown to an immense size. The spectators, to whom golf was something metaphysical and Jones its spiritual leader, didn't care what Jones shot, they just wanted to see him do it. His caddie, a young man of no more than twenty, had not seen Jones play since he was just a lad and Jones an untouchable giant. The young man was speechless from the aplomb with which Jones, now a near-legend, was treating this most sacred of all golf courses and yet walking among these people to whom it was sacred as though he were an archbishop at a parish picnic— shaking every hand that was outstretched to him, smiling at those who couldn't reach him, beaming with benevolence toward all.

The eighth hole is a par-three, 178 yards long, with a bunker to the left-front of the green. The flagstick that day was tucked behind a mound to the right. Jones plucked a four-iron from his bag, teed up his ball, and then, with that authoritative address that flowered into a backswing before the eye could notice, rifled a shot toward the bunker. The ball faded ever so feathery to the right, tucking itself, as it snuck toward the flagstick, behind the mound, plainly close enough for still another birdie.

The gallery roared approval. At St. Andrews, as nowhere else, they know a shot of uncommon grace when they see one.

As Jones stepped aside to let Auchterlonie play, he slipped the four-iron back into his bag, folded his arms over his chest, and stared shyly at the ground. His young caddie spoke, under his breath, for the first time since they had walked off the first tee together.

The look on his face then came back to Jones, twenty-two years later, the instant he had pushed himself to his feet to speak in that hall after the provost had made him a freeman of this Royal Burgh he loved so much. And the words that caddie spoke moved Jones more than all the millions upon millions that had been written about him.

As the gallery cheered, the caddie whispered to Jones, "Aye, you're a wonder, sir. A wonder."

AFTERWORD

This book is not the official biography of Bobby Jones, the official history of the Augusta National Golf Club, or the official chronicle of The Masters Tournaments. But it is the *authorized* version of all three. There is a difference.

An "official" book would have included virtually everything we know about all three subjects, and consequently would have been at least five times as long as this one, probably pedantically so, and as such would have spoiled the purposes of the enterprise.

The primary purpose was to tell, in story form, how Augusta National and hence The Masters Tournament came to be what they are, this for the many thousands of people who have for so long loyally watched Masters Tournaments on television and read accounts of them in newspapers without ever having had the opportunity to go to the club to see a tournament in person. I did not want the book to take as long to read as would going to Augusta National to watch The Masters actually take place.

The secondary purpose of the book was to bring Bobby Jones into proper historical focus, for without Jones—the *real* Bobby Jones—there never could have been an Augusta National and hence The Masters Tournament. For the overwhelming part, what I have interpreted about Jones was based on countless but nonetheless memorable hours of one-on-one conversations with him between 1958, when I had started editing the first issues of *Golf Magazine*, and his death thirteen years later.

Those conversations took place at the Vanderbilt Hotel in New York City, at *tête-à-têtes* in his Atlanta office that often stretched into cocktails and sandwiches across his desk, and during almost daily visits to his cottage at Augusta National during Masters Tournaments when, after he became too crippled to ride in a cart, I served as his "legman," reporting back to him what I had seen on the course that he could not gather from the scoreboard outside his living-room window.

Taking into account that there was twenty-three years difference in our ages, I have never known precisely why he extended to me such courtesies, especially since during those years he was patently weary of talking over old times. I can only presume now that he was passing some sort of golf torch to me, with the unstated chance that I might some day somehow get down accurately in book form just who he was and what he was like, all this so that generations of golfers yet to come might know.

This book, then, was purposely written with the memory of Bob Jones looking over my shoulder. I'm sure that a lot of what I have written is praise that his innate modesty would have found embarrassing. It's a risk I was willing to take. If you had admired him as much as I did, you would have taken that risk, too.

For this authorized version, I am indebted to Hord W. Hardin, chairman of both Augusta National and The Masters Tournament, for opening to me archives of both the club and the tournament to such an extent that what I have written can be construed as "official" anyway, especially since every word I then wrote pertaining to Augusta National and The Masters Tournament was checked beyond all reasonable doubt by Kathryn Murphy, executive secretary of The Masters Tournament. For this scrutiny, readers as well as myself owe Mrs. Murphy special thanks; there has been a great deal of nonsense written about the club and the tournament that has now gone up in smoke because of her help.

Much help was also given without hesitation by Col. David Davis, the tournament director; James Armstrong, manager of Augusta National; and Mrs. Hazel Salmon, also of the tournament staff, a woman who operates the pressroom so obligingly that she was once given a special award by the Golf Writers Association of America, an honor rare for a woman.

The photographs were selected for their historical value and not just for illustrative purposes; this book was not published just to decorate a coffee table. So, many of the pictures will have been seen elsewhere by some readers. My thanks for running them down and keeping track of them go to Jean Bowden. Thanks also go to Ken Bowden, her husband, who refereed the syntax and challenged the accuracy of the manuscript. It helped the authority of the book considerably that Ken is himself a writer, an editor, and an expert on golf.

Much of what isn't in historical books about The Masters I learned firsthand by going to the tournament as a writer all but continuously beginning in 1948. During that time, I discussed both the club and the tournament with every personage mentioned in this book who was still alive, and a number of others who are not mentioned. One who comes immediately to mind is Ike Grainger, the nonagenarian former president of the USGA and long-time Augusta National member. The late Jerome Franklin, the last surviving charter member of Augusta National, is another. But there were countless others whom I unhappily can't remember, so many were there. But they know who they are, and so my apologies to them as well as my thanks.

The biographical information on Clifford Roberts came, after many fruitless phone calls elsewhere, unexpectedly and wholeheartedly from his nephew, Kenneth Roberts, of Carmichael, California, to whom all of Augusta National should now be indebted, so wrapped in mystery were Cliff Roberts's early years even to members who had known him for half a century. And it must be noted that no such book as this could have been even begun without Roberts's random memoirs, which he so thoughtfully wrote down and which Doubleday & Company so wisely published not long before his death.

The information on General Eisenhower I owe in part to Stephen E. Ambrose, professor of history at the University of New Orleans and the General's definitive biographer.

I was lucky enough in my formative days as a golf writer to have known both O. B. Keeler and Grantland Rice, who knew the early years of both Augusta National and The Masters Tournaments better than anybody then or since. They also knew Bobby Jones as no one else ever has. I am thankful to the memory of both for having been so often kind enough to tell me years ago a lot about Jones over a few drinks—quite a few. Notwithstanding, the inspiration for this book came very soberly from those two pathfinders of early sportswriting in America.

—*Charles Price*
Wellington, Florida
January 1986

BIBLIOGRAPHY

Ambrose, Stephen E. *Eisenhower*. New York: Simon and Schuster, 1983.

Drosnin, Michael. *Citizen Hughes*. New York: Holt, Rinehart and Winston, 1985.

Jones, Robert T., Jr. *Down the Fairway*. New York: Minton Balch & Co., 1926.

——. *Golf Is My Game*. Garden City, N.Y.: Doubleday & Co., 1960.

——. *Bobby Jones on Golf*. Edited by Charles Price. Garden City, NY., Doubleday & Co., 1966.

Keeler, O. B. *The Bobby Jones Story*. Edited by Grantland Rice. Atlanta: Tupper and Love, 1959.

Leshan, Lawrence, and Margenau, Henry. *Einstein's Space & Van Gogh's Sky*. New York: Macmillan Publishing Co., Collier Books, 1982.

Mackenzie, Alister. *Golf Architecture*. London: Simpkin, Marshall, Hamilton & Kent, 1920.

Miller, Dick. *Triumphant Journey*. New York: Holt, Rinehart and Winston, 1980.

Price, Charles. *The World of Golf*. New York: Random House, 1962.

——. *Golfer at Large*. New York: Atheneum, 1984.

——, ed. *The American Golfer*. New York: Random House, 1964.

Rice, Grantland. *The Best of Grantland Rice*. Selected by Dave Camerer. New York: Franklin Watts, 1963.

Roberts, Clifford. *The Story of the Augusta National Golf Club*. Garden City, N.Y.: Doubleday & Co., 1976.

Schonberg, Harold C. *The Lives of the Great Composers*. New York: W.W. Norton & Co., 1970.

Wind, Herbert Warren. *The Story of American Golf*. New York: Farrar, Straus and Co., 1948.

INDEX

A. G. Spalding & Bros., 83, 139, 144

Adair, Perry, 58

Ahrens, Don, 192

Allen, George, 170–71

amateur/professional status, 211–12, 219

American Golfer, The, 19, 75, 83

Anderson, Willie, 208

Arkell, Bartlett, 118

Armour, Tommy, 14, 16, 55, 114, 119, 131, 154

Atkinson, Harry, 104–5

Auchterlonie, Laurie, 66

Auchterlonie, Willie, 222, 223

Augusta Country Club, 9, 98, 101

Augusta Fleetwood Hotel, 89–92, 101

Augusta, Georgia, plans for golf club in, 8–9, 92–95

Augusta National Golf Club. *See also* Masters Tournament
  course design changes, 4–5, 117–18, 163–65, 213–14
  creation of, 3–10, 32, 33, 35, 39, 87–116
  during World War II, 155, 159–61
  membership of, 6, 120–21, 160

Augusta National Invitation, 117–28

Ball, John, Jr., 4

Ballesteros, Steve, 6

Barber, Edward J., 160

Barber, Jerry, 187

Barrett, Thomas, Jr., 95, 100, 101, 130–31

Belloc, Hilaire, 105

Berckmans, Allie, 118–19

Berckmans, Louis Alphonse, 89, 118

Berckmans, Louis Mathieu Edouard, 87, 88

Berckmans, Prosper Julius Alphonse, 87, 88–89

Bing Crosby's Pro-Am, 162

Bobby Jones on Golf, 53, 178

Bolt, Tommy, 187

Boros, Julius, 187

Bourne, Alfred S., 95, 99, 102

Braid, James, 4, 199

Brewer, Gay, 205

British Amateur champions, 13–14, 17–18, 21, 27, 49, 140, 144
  Jones's British Amateur championships, 64–69

British Open champions, 12, 43, 59, 132, 140, 179, 184, 187, 199, 200, 201, 207
  Jones's British Open championships, 12, 27, 59, 69–70

Brown, Francis, 18
Brown, John Arthur, 122
Burke, Billy, 21, 132
Burke, Jack, Jr., 150, 187, 188, 193, 197
Burkemo, Walter, 187
Burns, Jimmy, 205

caddies, 45, 74
Cobb, Ty, 62
Coe, Charlie, 199–200, 202
Cooper, Harry, 132
Corcoran, Fred, 153–54
Cruickshank, Bobby, 63, 132
Cypress Point Golf Club, California, 18–19, 35

Darwin, Bernard, 15, 51, 83
Demaret, Jimmy, 145, 149–50, 154, 166, 183, 184, 187, 210
Dey, Joseph C., Jr., 75
Diegel, Leo, 132
Down the Fairway (Jones and Keeler), 59
Dudley, Ed, 119, 171
Dunlap, Gibby, 25
Dunphy, Chris, 122
Dutra, Olin, 132

Egan, H. Chandler, 21–22, 31
Eisenhower, Dwight D., 71, 158, 166, 169–73
Espinosa, Al, 15–16, 56
Evans, Charles "Chick," Jr., 45–46, 57, 144

Farrell, Johnny, 16, 132
Finlay, Phil, 18
Finsterwald, Dow, 200
Fitzgerald, F. Scott, 39–40, 58, 95
Ford, Doug, 193, 197
Fruitlands Nurseries, 87–88, 101

Gallico, Paul, 60
Gardner, Bob, 31
Ghezzi, Vic, 150
    golf clubs
    hickory shafts, 66
    Jones's Spalding designs, 83–85
    steel-shaft, 4
    switch from hickory to steel shafts, 6, 132, 146–48
Golf Illustrated, 64
Golf Is My Game (Jones), 178
golf swing
    Jones's, 15, 51–52, 53
    Vardon's, 12
Golf World, 211
golf-course architects, 5, 9–10, 11, 18, 19, 31, 32–33, 35–36, 92, 106–16
Goodman, Johnny, 23–25, 26, 27–29, 31, 33, 106, 130, 144, 209
Gould, Alan, 151
Grand Slam, 37, 61–76, 80, 136, 152, 158–59, 180
Grant, Douglas, 11, 22
Gruenther, Alfred, 171
Guldahl, Ralph, 147–49
Gunn, Watts, 27

Hagen, Walter, 12, 14, 22, 42, 43, 45, 46, 47, 49, 55, 59–60, 131, 132, 140, 183, 206, 208
Hammack, Simk, 155, 159
Harbert, Chick, 187
Hardin, Hord W., 216–17
Harlow, Bob, 211, 212
Harmon, Claude, 166
Harrison, E. J. "Dutch," 188
Havemeyer, Theodore, 78–79
Herbert, Jay, 187
Hilton, Harold, 4
Hines, Jimmy, 132
historical figures, 40, 41, 70–71

Hogan, Ben, 6, 22, 43, 47, 154,
   158, 202
   Masters Tournaments, 145,
      147, 148, 149, 151, 161–63,
      165–66, 184–85, 187,
      188–92, 210
Homans, Gene, 25, 73
Hughes, Howard, 26
Hutchison, Jock, 179

Jacobs, Tommy, 205
James, William, 46
Jamieson, Andrew, 27
Johnston, Harrison "Jimmy," 24,
   31, 64, 67–68, 69
Jones, Clara (mother), 76
Jones, Mary Malone (wife), 58,
   63, 69, 74
Jones, Robert P. (father), 55, 56
Jones, Robert Trent (architect),
   164–65
Jones, Robert Tyre, Jr. (Bobby)
   amateur championships at
      Pebble Beach, 12–13,
      16–18, 25–26, 27–29
   amateur/professional status,
      211–12, 219
   Augusta National Invitation,
      117–28
   British Amateur champi-
      onships, 49, 64–69
   British Open championships,
      12, 27, 59, 69–70
   career, 39–60
   columns/publications by, 53,
      59, 83
   and creation of Augusta
      National, 32–33, 35, 39,
      92–94, 98–116, 117–18
   death of, 217–19
   Eisenhower and, 169, 171–73
   first national championship,
      29–31

freeman ceremony at St.
   Andrews, 220–23
golf clubs designs, 83–85
golf swing/stance, 15, 51–52,
   53
Grand Slam, 61–76, 80, 136,
   158–59
Havemeyer Trophy to, 78–79
illness, 173–78, 180–81
injuries, 72–73
instructional films series,
   82–83
law practice, 50, 81, 85–86
Mackenzie and, 31, 33, 36,
   106, 108–10
and Masters Tournament, 39,
   130, 131, 133–36, 138–39,
   140, 143, 149, 151–52, 159,
   160, 161, 163, 164, 166–67,
   178–79, 198
media coverage of, 29, 73, 74,
   75–76, 80, 81, 94–95, 108–9,
   135, 151–52
in the military, 155–59
national titles, 22–23, 48–49
on Nicklaus, 205–6
parades for, 70–71, 104–5
playing style, 14–15
retirement, 31–32, 77–86
United States Amateur championships, 13–14, 25–26,
   27–29, 49, 72, 73–75, 78–80
United States Open championships, 12, 15–16, 25, 26,
   27, 44, 48, 49, 59, 71–72,
   166
Jones, W. Alton "Pete," 170

Keeler, Oscar Bane "O. B.," 53,
   59, 127
   and creation of Augusta
      National, 93–94, 103–4, 105
   and Grand Slam, 61, 63, 69,
      75, 80

on Jones's career, 19, 27, 28, 29, 31, 33, 35, 37
and Jones's retirement, 77–78
Keiser, Herman, 162
Kelland, Clarence Budington, 83
Key, Dorias, 96
Key, Rebecca Scott, 95

Laffoon, Ky, 132
Lane, William H., 215–16
Lapham, Henry, 27
Lapham, Louis, 18, 19–20
Lapham, Roger, 18
Lardner, Ring, 83
Leonard, Stan, 194
Little, Lawson, 21, 22, 23, 31, 140, 144
Littler, Gene, 187, 205
Locke, Bobby, 166, 206
Los Angeles Open, 145, 161–62

Macfarlane, Willie, 56, 119, 132
Mackenzie, Alister, 34
   creation and design of Augusta National, 33, 35, 92, 106–16, 170
   death of, 117
   Jones and, 31, 33, 36, 106, 108–10
Mackenzie-built golf courses, 18, 19, 29, 35–36
Maiden, Stewart, 50–51
Mangrum, Lloyd, 150, 154, 162, 166, 187, 188
Marshall, Jean, 177
Marshall, Walton H., 95, 97, 98, 99, 102, 120, 130, 159
Marston, Max, 26
Masters Tournament (Augusta National Golf Club), 4, 5, 6–7, 8, 129–52, 159–61, 178–80
   Augusta National Invitation becomes, 124, 125, 130–32, 139–40, 149

green jacket, 179–80
guidelines for, 139
Jones and creation of, 33, 39
as a major championship, 183–98
method for inviting contestants, 44
postwar, 160–63, 165–67
Series Badges for, 7–8
sponsors for, 192
television broadcasts of, 192–97
tournament innovations, 209–13
Mayer, Dick, 194
McLeod, Fred, 179
McSpaden, Harold "Jug," 132, 154
Middlecroft, Cary, 187, 188, 194
Miller, Wendell P., 108
modern golf, beginnings of, 4
Monroe, Jay, 127–28, 138

national championship golf, 47
Nelson, Byron, 6, 22, 43, 154, 161–62, 165, 187, 210
   Masters Tournaments, 140, 145, 147, 148, 149, 150, 151
Neville, Jack, 11, 22
Nicklaus, Jack, 6, 47, 60, 199, 202–8, 209, 213–14

Ochs, Adolph S., 90
Ouimet, Francis, 22, 26, 31, 33, 42, 44, 45, 46, 55, 57, 144
"over-and-under" method of posting scores, 212

Palmer, Arnold, 6, 22, 60, 172, 193–97, 198, 199, 200–202, 207, 208, 209
Parks, Sam, 132
Patton, William Joseph, 187–92